T0289566

Christmas in Nevada

Christmas
in Nevada

PATRICIA D. CAFFERATA

UNIVERSITY OF NEVADA PRESS

Reno & Las Vegas

University of Nevada Press, Reno, Nevada 89557 USA
www.unpress.nevada.edu
Copyright © 2014 by University of Nevada Press
All rights reserved
Manufactured in the United States of America
Design by Kathleen Szawiola

Library of Congress Cataloging-in-Publication Data

Cafferata, Patricia D., 1940-
Christmas in Nevada / Patricia D. Cafferata.
pages   cm
Includes index.
ISBN 978-0-87417-949-1 (cloth : alk. paper) —
ISBN 978-0-87417-950-7 (e-book)
1. Christmas—Nevada—History. I. Title.
GT4986.N37C34 2014
394.2663—dc23   2014009615

The paper used in this book meets the requirements of
American National Standard for Information Sciences—
Permanence of Paper for Printed Library Materials,
ANSI/NISO Z39.48-1992 (R2002). Binding materials were
selected for strength and durability.

FIRST PRINTING
23   22   21   20   19   18   17
5   4   3   2

FRONTISPIECE: Christmas tree. Copyright ©iStockPhoto, h2hines

FOR MY FAMILY,
especially my husband, Treat;
our children and their spouses,
Elisa, Farrell and Caren, and Reynolds and Becky;
and our grandchildren,
Brendan, Morgan, Kenton and Kelley,
Dean and Quinn,
and Taylor, Henry, and Grace

Contents

Preface   *xiii*

Map of Nevada   *xx*

Introduction: No Place Like Nevada for the Holidays   1

"A Christmas Carol," Nevada Style: Story About a
Mysterious Piano Player, by Sam Davis
CARSON CITY AND LINCOLN COUNTY   4

Preachers and Presents Everywhere: Christmas on the Comstock
STOREY COUNTY   11

Mark Twain's Mentor in Virginia City:
Comedian Artemus Ward's Christmas Performances
STOREY COUNTY   14

O Tannenbaum! O Tannenbaum! Reno's Famous and
Infamous Christmas Trees
WASHOE COUNTY   16

Waltzing Through the Sagebrush:
Victorian Christmases in Humboldt County
HUMBOLDT COUNTY   20

Reno Churches Competed for Attendance:
Trees and Santa Were the Enticements
WASHOE COUNTY   23

The "Nevergreen" Trees: Tonopah's Quirky Christmas Decorations

NYE COUNTY   25

Sleigh Tracks in Silver Peak: Alice's Proof of Santa's Visit

ESMERALDA COUNTY   28

PHOTOGRAPHS: *Early 1900s*   *29*

Happy Holidays in Las Vegas:
Community Clubs Provide Merry Celebrations

CLARK COUNTY   37

Christmas in a Tomb: Miners Imprisoned for Forty-Five Days

WHITE PINE COUNTY   40

Catholics in the Congregational Church:
A Gift in the Spirit of Christmas

WASHOE COUNTY   43

O Christmas Tree: Nevada's Oldest Growing Community Tree

CARSON CITY   46

The Stovall Kids "Planted" a Forest:
Christmas in Goldfield in the 1920s

ESMERALDA COUNTY   50

Josephine and the Scary Santa: A Jarbidge Christmas

ELKO COUNTY   53

Christmas Comes to Yerington: Plans and Surprises

LYON COUNTY   54

The Richest Christmas: Snowbound on the Swallow Ranch in 1923

WHITE PINE COUNTY   57

Churches and Courthouse Trees: Eureka's Holiday Spirit in the 1920s

EUREKA COUNTY 60

Santa Claus and Yule Missa: Danish and American Christmases

EUREKA COUNTY 63

Santa Claus Rang the Doorbell: Christmas in Lovelock

PERSHING COUNTY 65

"It's a Christmas Tree": Basque Immigrants and
an American Tradition, by Robert Laxalt

CARSON CITY 67

PHOTOGRAPHS: *1920s–1930s* 71

A Christmas Tree Tradition Born in the Depression:
Santa Distributed Nineteen Hundred Stockings

CHURCHILL COUNTY 77

Santa Claus Comes to Las Vegas: Christmas in a Growing Town

CLARK COUNTY 79

The Christmas Gal: Shirley Biglieri Lived for Christmas

EUREKA AND WASHOE COUNTIES 81

Santa Claus's Will: An Incredible Gift to Needy Children

CARSON CITY AND LYON COUNTY 83

Three Days to Celebrate: Boulder City Christmas in 1931

CLARK COUNTY 86

"Merry Christmas, Darlings!": Old Ornaments and Glamour Girl Gifts

WASHOE COUNTY 87

Santa Claus and the Nativity Story: Tahoe Indian Parish's Events

CARSON CITY AND WASHOE AND DOUGLAS COUNTIES   90

Enchanting Pogonip: Northern Nevada's Frozen Fog

WASHOE COUNTY   91

A Nevada Christmas Smell: A Pilot Asked Santa for Sagebrush

DOUGLAS COUNTY   93

Nevada's Piñon and Tumbleweed Trees: Leila Remembers
the Tonopah Trees

NYE COUNTY   94

Dining in the Governor's Mansion: The List Family's Christmases

CARSON CITY AND WASHOE COUNTY   96

Richard Bryan's Christmas Celebrations: Unique Timing and Presents

CLARK COUNTY AND CARSON CITY   99

PHOTOGRAPHS: 1940s–1950s   103

Angel Without Wings: Mother Made Christmas Magical

CLARK COUNTY   113

A Toy Factory in Verdi: An Earthquake Destroyed Santa's Workshop

WASHOE COUNTY   115

Honey Cake Holiday Houses: German Christmas Goodies
and Decorations

WASHOE COUNTY   117

Christmas at Sunny Acres: Special Treats for the Children

CARSON CITY AND CHURCHILL COUNTY   119

The "Santa Spirit": Celebrating Christmas Year-Round

CLARK COUNTY   122

Tasha's Christmases in Tonopah: Piñon Pines and Serbian Meals

NYE COUNTY   124

The Christmas Flood of 1955: The Holiday Spirit Remains

WASHOE COUNTY   126

Christmas in Black Springs: Carrie Townsell's Love of the Season

WASHOE COUNTY   129

Nevada Christmas Cards: The Records of the Melton and
Ireland Families

WASHOE AND CLARK COUNTIES   133

Christmas Ornaments in Mina: A Prescott Family Tradition

MINERAL COUNTY   136

Christmas Tamales: Adriana's Mexican and
Nevada Holiday Traditions

WASHOE COUNTY   138

Opportunity Village's Magical Forest and Santa Run:
Las Vegas Events Enrich Lives

CLARK COUNTY   141

"Christmas Trees on the Mountain," by Molly Flagg Knudtsen

LANDER COUNTY   143

"Is There a Santa Claus?":
Nevada Attorney General Brian McKay's Answer

CARSON CITY   144

No More Charlie Brown Trees:
Claytee White's Perfect Christmas Tradition

CLARK COUNTY   146

Winter Gardens in Las Vegas: Bellagio Las Vegas's Wonderland

CLARK COUNTY   147

Sharp Needles and Soft Lights: Ethel M Chocolates' Holiday Garden

CLARK COUNTY   150

PHOTOGRAPHS: *1960s to the Present*   *153*

Nevada's Willow Reindeer Herd: Children Handcraft the Animals

CARSON CITY   163

Reno's Santa Pub Crawl: Thousands Join the Fun

WASHOE COUNTY   164

Elko's "Twelve Days of Christmas": Several Weeks of Spirited Events

ELKO COUNTY   167

Governor Brian Sandoval's Executive Order:
Message on Assisting Santa

CARSON CITY   169

A Few Additional Nevada Holiday Events   173

Index   *175*

Preface

THIS BOOK RECOUNTS the interesting, touching, and fun ways that
Nevadans have celebrated Christmas, from before statehood to the present day. I was inspired to write this history of my unique state because
Christmas has always been my favorite time of the year. My appreciation
for this holiday is deeply rooted in my own family memories of this season, and many of these might be familiar to anyone who grew up in this
state.

My earliest memories of Christmas in Nevada are from the 1950s. A
few weeks before Christmas, my mother, Barbara, and (step) father, Ken
Dillon, as well as my younger brothers, Mike, Kenny, and Tommy, and I
drove to a tree lot in town to select a tree. Our favorite trees were bushy,
but not piñons. After looking at all the available trees and much discus-
sion, we purchased the absolutely best evergreen tree.

The trees I most vividly remember were the ones we put up during
my high school years, when we lived on Newlands Circle in Reno. When
I was in college, our sister, Susie, was born, and as she grew older, she
joined in our holiday activities. Our dad erected the tree in a corner of the
large front hall, and the scent of pine filled the house. We decorated our
Christmas tree with colorful, fragile store-bought glass-ball ornaments
and lights. A few presents appeared under the tree before Christmas, but
Santa Claus left his presents on Christmas Eve, long after we had gone to
bed.

Early Christmas morning Mike and I rushed to the tree before anyone
else was awake and ripped off the paper from all of our presents in minutes. The wonder, surprise, and excitement were soon over. Later, our
mom moved the Christmas tree to the rumpus room in the basement.

Mike and I could not make the trip down two flights of stairs as fast, but by then we were not as eager because we had helped Santa to assemble the gifts for Kenny, Tommy, and Susie. Yet we were delighted to be in on the secret gifts they would discover in the morning. Best of all, our own presents were still a surprise.

As a grown-up, I started a Christmas tradition in 1960 that has continued for more than fifty years. When I was in college and Treat Cafferata (my soon-to-be husband) was in medical school, I knitted him a two-foot green-and-white-striped Christmas stocking and embroidered it in red with his initials and the year. After we were married in 1961, I continued the stocking tradition when we became parents. I knitted stockings for our daughters, Elisa and Farrell, and son, Reynolds, for their first Christmases. And when the kids married, I knitted stockings for their spouses, including the year each one joined the family. When the grandchildren began to arrive, our daughter Elisa knitted a stocking for each new arrival. The socks are striped and are made with red, green, and white yarn. All the stockings are similar, but no two are alike. All are different sizes, but none is tiny. As far as the kids are concerned, the best feature is how the socks stretch as presents are loaded into them, leaving room on top for more presents. The stockings are laid out by the fireplace and are the first presents opened on Christmas morning.

Cutting our own Christmas tree became a family activity in the 1970s. We joined thousands of other Nevadans and obtained a Bureau of Land Management tree tag for one dollar. We drove to the Pine Nut Mountains in Douglas County to find the perfect piñon pine tree. The best trees seemed to be located high in areas covered in deep snow.

On these searches everyone in the family bundled up, but they were still cold in the freezing weather. We wore high boots, yet our feet got wet as we trudged around to find a tree we liked. Their size was always deceptive; for some reason, out on the mountain the trees seemed smaller than they actually were. Sometimes, Treat had to cut off the bottom of the tree when we got it home because it was taller than the ceiling, so he could not set it up in the house. Unfortunately, the best-looking trees, perfectly symmetrical, had two trunks. The challenge was to make sure not to pick one of those trees. If we made a mistake and cut a tree with dual trunks, when we got it home the piñon looked like a puffy bush, not a Christmas tree.

Treat had to avoid the piñon's sharp, prickly needles as he sawed down the tree. Gloves were a necessity because carrying the tree back to the car or truck was a sticky activity due to the tree's heavy pitch. The pungent smell of the piñon that filled the house when we set it up made the cold, wet trip worthwhile.

One year in the 1970s, a Cafferata cousin gave the family a handmade eight-foot white plywood snowman for a yard decoration. He wore a green cap and held a gigantic red-and-white-striped candy cane. A few years later, Treat fashioned a giant snow lady and two smaller snow children from plywood sheets. Elisa painted them white and dressed them in red and green hats to match the giant snowman. Treat put up these figures year after year, usually in a snowstorm during Thanksgiving weekend. When Reynolds was in high school, he graduated from Treat's assistant to the chief installer of the snow family and other outside lawn decorations.

Over the years, as the weather took its toll, Elisa painted and repainted the snow family. If their stands broke, Farrell repaired the figures so they stood tall on our lawn. We displayed the snow family every Christmas season for more than forty years in Reno, and Farrell now erects them on her front lawn in Carson City.

These stories are how my family and I have celebrated Christmas. Other families and people have developed their own traditions, and this book is about how some Nevadans, their families, and their communities observe the holiday.

Just like Christmas morning, readers will encounter many surprises in *Christmas in Nevada.* To make it easy for the readers, the book is organized chronologically, beginning with features about past Christmases from before statehood in 1858 to Governor Brian Sandoval's executive order in 2011. The chronicles include many events in Nevada's mining camps, ranches, and big cities. The accounts also include delightful personal stories of Nevadans. The information for the earlier pieces was taken from journals, newspaper accounts, and other historical records. The later stories were based on interviews with Nevadans about their holiday memories.

The book, however, does not need to be read from the first page to the last. The stories may be read in any order that pleases the reader, as if the book were a collection of short stories. Each story begins with a headnote to introduce the reader to the location and characters and to highlight the importance of the account.

Every year families, communities, and organizations hold hundreds of holiday events in December. Unfortunately, not all of these could be included in this book, so only a few of these activities are listed at the end of the book.

Stories about the past require tremendous amounts of research before a word is written down. I could not have written these Christmas stories without the assistance of the following people. Michael Maher, Heidi Englund, and Arlene Laferry at the Nevada Historical Society; Chris Driggs and Natasha Faillers at the Nevada State Archives; and friend Don Drake helped me with locating sources and materials. Sharon Quinn and my daughter Elisa Cafferata spent hours reviewing and editing the manuscript. Public services and photographs assistant Delores Brownlee of the University of Nevada, Las Vegas, University Libraries, Department of Special Collections, and media specialist Ginny Poehling for the News Bureau of the Las Vegas Convention and Visitors Authority found some of the historic photographs of Las Vegas. Marilyn Melton and Jeanne Ireland allowed me to use their family Christmas cards. Richard Bryan, David Russell, and Helen Townsell-Parker allowed me to use photographs of their families. Jerry Fenwick and Neal Cobb permitted me to use some of their historic photographs. Two artists contributed their artwork: Ruth Hilts permitted me to use her watercolor of the Gold Hill Hotel, while Frank Ozaki drew the map of Nevada for the book.

I wrote the memoirs section after interviewing the following Nevadans about their unique Christmas traditions. In alphabetical order, they include Dick Belaustegui, Phyllis Anker Bendure, Clyde Biglieri, Richard Bryan, Adriana Guzmán Fralick, Leila Wolfe Fuson, Cherrie Prescott George, Tasha Tomany Hall, Nancy Murray Harkess, Harold Jacobsen,

Bob List, Kathy Geary List, Carrie Townsell, Helen Townsell-Parker, Clay-tee White, and Valerie Wiener. Marilyn Fuetsch shared her mother's story from her diary.

I thank them all for their patience and time in recounting their personal and family histories.

Most of all, I thank Matt Becker, the editor who guided me through the process, Kathleen Szawiola, the design and production manager who designed the book, and the University of Nevada Press for publishing these Christmas stories.

Christmas in Nevada

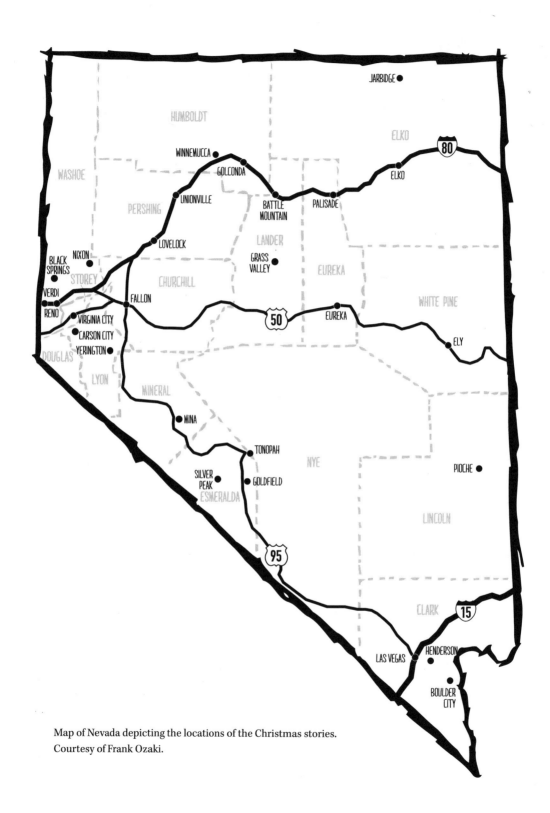

Map of Nevada depicting the locations of the Christmas stories.
Courtesy of Frank Ozaki.

Introduction
No Place Like Nevada for the Holidays

The earliest inhabitants of the Great Basin (an area that includes Nevada), the Native American tribes the Paiute, Shoshone, Washoe, and Goshute, did not celebrate Christmas until after the settlers brought their European culture and Christianity to the area. Since the founding of the state of Nevada in 1864, the people who settled here created the state's holiday culture and its unique Christmas traditions. Yet just like the people in other states, Nevadans believe in Santa Claus and listen for his jingling sleigh bells, hang stockings, decorate pungent-smelling pine trees, and festively wrap their presents in colorful holiday paper. These traditions remind residents of their own childhood Christmases and promote feelings of hope, anticipation, and excitement.

Long before Nevada's statehood, ol' Saint Nick had established his place in American culture. The Dutch brought their Sinterklaas when they came to the New World. He eventually became the familiar Santa Claus Nevadans know today. Along with Santa, evergreen trees, and presents, the pioneers celebrated their Victorian Christmas traditions by holding dances and parties, singing carols and other holiday songs, preparing special foods, and attending merry entertainment.

In 1869 a skeptical *Humboldt Register* reporter opined that people were not supposed to be "out in this wilderness, sage-brush country." He believed that although the holiday celebrations could not approximate anything near what they were like "at home," the people would *perhaps* enjoy it somewhat. Nothing could be further from the truth. From the beginning, Nevadans kept their favorite Christmas traditions, and Santa Claus never stopped making his evening rounds to the delight of all.

Santa's challenge has always been to get to every home on Christmas Eve, even in the most faraway places in Nevada—the seventh largest in land size of the fifty states. Nevada's motto, Battle Born, indicates the state joined the Union during the Civil War (1861–65). Days before he completed his term as president of the United States, James Buchanan signed the act that established the Nevada Territory on March 2, 1861. The new territory was carved from the western side of the Utah Territory. After the residents adopted a state constitution in September 1864, President Abraham Lincoln signed the proclamation creating the State of Nevada on October 31, 1864.

In Carson City, the state capital, an evergreen tree was planted on the capitol grounds in 1876, and the tree has been decorated nearly every year since 1914. Many of the governors and their families have taken an active role in throwing the switch to light the town's tree. Santa and Mrs. Claus often stop by to deliver holiday treats to the children in town.

In the state's first sixty years, the discoveries of gold and silver in Storey, Humboldt, Eureka, Lander, and Lincoln Counties and other areas drew people to Nevada. At first the men in these mining camps created their own yuletide entertainment. As the men's wives and children arrived, towns sprang up and grew into sophisticated cities, where the churches, businesses, and community organizations arranged programs and held parties to celebrate the holiday.

As new ore bodies were discovered around the state, the miners abandoned the places where the ore had petered out and hurried to the new mines. From the beginning of the twentieth century to 1915, prospectors rushed to several major mining regions, such as Tonopah (Nye County) and Goldfield (Esmeralda County) in central Nevada.

With the discovery of copper, White Pine County boomed from 1904 to 1921. After that the mining across the state declined and did not recover until the 1980s. At that time, because of new technology, gold mining in the northeastern counties of Eureka and Elko turned profitable again, and many people flocked to those areas.

In Washoe County, when the Central Pacific Railroad laid its tracks through the Truckee Meadows and created the city of Reno in 1868, the area became the transportation hub for the Virginia City mines. Because the major industries—mining and transportation—employed so many men, scores of families and single people moved to Reno. The town remained the major center of commercial activity in the state until the 1950s. Renoites created a yuletide tradition of erecting and decorating a community Christmas tree downtown. Santa and Mrs. Claus often visited the tree, to the delight of the kids in Reno.

In 1905 the San Pedro, Los Angeles & Salt Lake Railroad built a depot on its line in what would become Clark County, and the town of Las Vegas sprang up to service the railway's needs. During the height of the Great Depression, men and their families swept into Clark County for work when the federal government began the construction of the Hoover Dam in the 1930s. In 1931 the Nevada Legislature legalized gaming, sparking the expansion of the state's major industries—tourism and the hotel-casino business.

A combination of many events created Las Vegas's success—the railroad, the Hoover Dam, air-conditioning, and the legalization of gaming. Clark County rapidly grew and surpassed Washoe County's population by 1960. Today, most of the state's population lives in Clark County in the cities of Las Vegas, North Las Vegas, Henderson, and Boulder City.

In 1905 Santa Claus began appearing at the community Christmas tree erected on Fremont Street in Las Vegas to distribute gifts. Santa still appears downtown at the community Christmas tree and occasionally arrives on a zip line at the Fremont Street Experience, a pedestrian mall under a ninety-foot canopy downtown.

In counties such as Elko, Churchill, Douglas, Lyon, and Pershing, the ranchers and farmers discovered the areas were conducive to raising cattle and crops. Unlike the miners, these residents settled down to stay. The nature of agriculture required the families to make a long-term commitment to their communities and the state. In these towns the people celebrated Christmas with the Old World customs of dances, decorated trees, and special events. And, of course, Santa Claus managed to visit the homes of the little ones, no matter how far apart the ranches were.

From the earliest festivities in Virginia City and other mining camps to the first Christmas trees erected in Las Vegas and Reno, the Snowflake Festival in Elko, and the holiday memories of former governors Richard Bryan, Bob List, and others, Nevadans have long enjoyed this season in their own special ways. Stories about these historical delights, along with many others, await the reader in the pages that follow.

Merry Christmas!

"A Christmas Carol," Nevada Style:
Story About a Mysterious Piano Player

SAM DAVIS

Reporter Sam Davis worked for the Virginia City Chronicle in Storey County in the 1870s. After Henry Mighels, the publisher of the Nevada Appeal in Carson City, died, his widow, Nellie, hired Davis as the editor of her newspaper in 1880, and later they married. Davis served as the editor of that newspaper until he was elected state controller in 1898, a post he held until 1907.

In 1885 Davis wrote "A Christmas Carol," a story about a fictitious mining town in eastern Nevada. Others have edited and republished this yarn as "The First Piano in Camp." The story is printed below as he published it, including the inconsistent dates at the beginning and end of the story.

In 1858—it might have been five years earlier or later, this is not history for the public schools—there was a little camp about ten miles from Pioche, occupied by upwards of three hundred miners, every one of whom might have packed his prospecting implements and left for more inviting fields any time before sunset. When the day was over, these men did not rest from their labors, like the honest New England agriculturist, but sang, danced, gambled, and shot one other, as the mood seized them.

One evening the report spread along the main street (which was the only street) that three men had been killed at Silver Reef, and that the bodies were coming in. Presently a lumbering old conveyance labored up the hill, drawn by a couple of horses, well worn out with their pull. The cart contained a good-sized box, and no sooner did its outlines become visible through the glimmer of a stray light here and there, than it began to affect the idlers. Death always enforces respect, and even though no one had caught sight of the remains, the crowd gradually became subdued, and when the horses came to a stand-still, the cart was imme-diately surrounded. The driver, however, was not in the least impressed with the solemnity of his commission.

"All there?" asked one.

"Haven't examined. Guess so."

The driver filled his pipe and lit it as he continued:

"Wish the bones and load had gone over the grade."

A man who had been looking on stepped up to the man at once.

"I don't know who you have in that box, but if they happen to be any friends of mine, I'll lay you alongside."

"We can mighty soon see," said the teamster, coolly. "Just burst the lid off, and if they happen to be the men you want, I'm here."

The two men looked at each other for a moment, and then the crowd gathered a little closer, anticipating trouble.

"I believe that dead men are entitled to good treatment, and when you talk about hoping to see corpses go over a bank, all I have to say is, that it will be better for you if the late lamented ain't my friends."

"We'll open the box. I don't take back what I said, and if my language don't suit your ways of thinking, I guess I can stand it."

With those words the teamster began to pry up the lid. He got a board off, and then pulled out some rags. A strip of something dark, like rose-wood, presented itself.

"Eastern coffins, by thunder!" said several, and the crowd looked quite astonished.

Some more boards flew up, and the man who was ready to defend his friend's memory shifted his weapon a little. The cool manner of the teamster had so irritated him that he had made up his mind to pull his weapon at the first sight of the dead, even if the deceased was his worst and oldest enemy. Presently the whole of the box cover was off, and the teamster, clearing away the packing, revealed to the astonished group the top of something which puzzled all alike.

"Boys," said he, "this is a pianner!"

A general shout of laughter went up, and the man who had been so anxious to enforce respect for the dead muttered something about feel-ing dry, and the keeper of the nearest bar was several ounces better off by the time the boys had given the joke all the attention it called for.

Had a dozen dead men been in the box, their presence in the camp could not have occasioned half the excitement that the arrival of the lovely piano caused. By the next morning it was known that the instrument was to grace a hurdy-gurdy saloon owned by Tom Goskin, the leading gambler in the place. It took nearly a week to get this wonder on its legs, and the owner was the proudest individual in the State. It rose gradually from a recumbent to an upright position, amid a confusion of tongues, after the manner of the tower of Babel.

Of course, everybody knew just how such an instrument should be put up. One knew where the "off hind leg" should go, and another was posted on the "front piece."

Scores of men came to the place every day to assist.

"I'll put the bones in good order."

"If you want the wires turned up, I'm the boy."

"I've got music to feed it for a month."

Another brought a pair of blankets for a cover, and all took the liveliest interest in it. It was at last in a condition for business.

"It's been showin' its teeth all the week. We'd like to have it spit out something."

Alas! there wasn't a man to be found who could play upon the instrument. Goskin began to realize that he had a losing speculation on his hands. He had a fiddler, and a Mexican who thrummed a guitar. A pianist would have made his orchestra complete. One day a three-card monte player told a friend confidentially that he could "knock any amount of music out of the piano, if he only had it alone a few hours to get his hand in." This report spread about the camp, but on being questioned he vowed that he didn't know a note of music. It was noted, however, as a suspicious circumstance, that he often hung about the instrument, and looked upon it longingly, like a hungry man gloating over a beefsteak in a restaurant window. There was no doubt but that this man had music in his soul, perhaps in his finger-ends, but did not dare to make trial of his strength after the rules of harmony had suffered so many years of neglect. So the fiddler kept on with his jigs, and the Mexican pawed his discordant guitar, but no man had the nerve to touch that piano. There were, doubtless, scores of men in the camp who would have given ten ounces of gold-dust to have been half an hour alone with it, but every man's nerve shrank from the jeers which the crowd would shower upon him should his first attempt prove a failure. It got to be generally understood that the hand which first essayed to draw music from the keys must not slouch its work.

IT WAS CHRISTMAS EVE, and Goskin, according to his custom, had decorated his gambling hall with sprigs of mountain cedar and a shrub whose crimson berries did not seem a bad imitation of English holly. The piano was covered with evergreens, and all that was wanting to completely fill the cup of Goskin's contentment was a man to play that piano.

"Christmas night, and no piano-pounder," he said. "This is a nice country for a Christian to live in."

Getting a piece of paper, he scrawled the words:

> $20 Reward
>
> To a compitant Pianer Player.

This he stuck up on the music-rack, and, though the inscription glared at the frequenters of the room until midnight, it failed to draw any musician from his shell.

So the merry-making went on; the hilarity grew apace. Men danced and sang to the music of the squeaky fiddle and worn-out guitar, as the jolly crowd within tried to drown the howling of the storm without. Suddenly, they became aware of the presence of a white-haired man, crouching near the fire-place. His garments—such as were left—were wet with melting snow, and he had a half-starved, half-crazed expression. He held his thin, trembling hands toward the fire, and the light of the blazing wood made them almost transparent. He looked about him once in a while, as if in search of something, and his presence cast such a chill over the place that gradually the sound of the revelry was hushed, and it seemed that this waif of the storm had brought in with it all of the gloom and coldness of the warring elements. Goskin, mixing up a cup of hot egg-nogg, advanced and remarked cheerily:

"Here, stranger, brace up! This is the real stuff."

The man drained the cup, smacked his lips, and seemed more at home.

"Been prospecting, eh? Out in the mountains—caught in the storm? Lively night, this!"

"Pretty bad," said the man.

"Must feel pretty dry?"

The man looked at his steaming clothes and laughed, as if Goskin's remark was a sarcasm.

"How long out?"

"Four days."

"Hungry?"

The man rose up, and walking over to the lunch counter, fell to work upon some roast bear, devouring it like any wild animal would have done. As meat and drink and warmth began to permeate the stranger, he seemed to expand and lighten up. His features lost their pallor, and he grew more and more content with the idea that he was not in the grave. As he underwent these changes, the people about him got merrier and happier, and threw off the temporary feeling of depression which he had laid upon them.

"Do you always have your place decorated like this?" he finally asked of Goskin.

"This is Christmas Eve," was the reply.

The stranger was startled.

"December twenty-fourth, sure enough."

"That's the way I put it up, pard."

"When I was in England I always kept Christmas. But I had forgotten that this was the night. I've been wandering about in the mountains until I've lost track of the feasts of the church."

Presently his eye fell upon the piano.

"Where's the player?" he asked.

"Never had any," said Goskin, blushing at the expression.

"I used to play when I was young."

Goskin almost fainted at the admission.

"Stranger, do tackle it, and give us a tune! Nary had a man in this camp ever had the nerve to wrestle with that music-box." His pulse beat faster, for he feared that the man would refuse.

"I'll do the best I can," he said.

There was no stool, but seizing a candle-box, he drew it up and seated himself before the instrument. It only required a few seconds for a hush to come over the room.

"That old coon is going to give the thing a rattle."

The sight of a man at the piano was something so unusual that even the faro-dealer, who was about to take in a fifty-dollar bet on the tray, paused and did not reach for the money. Men stopped drinking, with the glasses at their lips. Conversation appeared to have been struck with a sort of paralysis, and cards were no longer shuffled.

The old man brushed back his long, white locks, looked up to the ceiling, half closed his eyes, and in a mystic sort of reverie passed his fingers over the keys. He touched but a single note, yet the sound thrilled the room. It was the key to his improvisation, and as he wove his chords together the music laid its spell upon every ear and heart. He felt his way along the keys, like a man treading uncertain paths; but he gained confidence as he progressed, and presently bent to his work like a master. The instrument was not in exact tune, but the ears of his audience, through long disuse, did not detect anything radically wrong. They heard a succession of grand chords, a suggestion of paradise, melodies here and there, and it was enough.

"See him counter with his left!" said one old rough, enraptured.

"He calls the turn every time on the upper end of the board," responded a man with a stack of chips in his hand.

The player wandered off into the old ballads they had heard at home. All the sad and melancholy, and touching songs that came up like dreams of childhood, this unknown player drew from the keys. His hands kneaded their hearts like dough, and squeezed out the tears as from a wet sponge. As the strains flowed one upon the other, they saw their homes of the long ago reared again; they were playing once more where the apple blossoms sank through the soft air to join the violets on the green turf of the old New England States; they saw the glories of the Wisconsin maples and the haze of the Indian summer, blending their hues together; they recalled the heather of Scottish hills, the white cliffs of Britain, and heard the sullen roar of the sea, as it beat upon their memories, vaguely. Then come all the old Christmas carols, such as they had sung in church thirty years before; the subtle music that brings up the glimmer of wax tapers, the solemn shrines, the evergreens, holly, mistletoe, and surpliced choirs. Then the remorseless performer planted his final stab in every heart with "Home, Sweet Home."

When the player ceased, the crowd slunk away from him. There was no more revelry and devilment left in his audience. Each man wanted to sneak off to his cabin and write the old folks a letter. The day was breaking as the last man left the place, and the player, laying his head down on the piano, fell asleep.

"I say, pard," said Goskin, "don't you want a little rest?"

"I feel tired," the old man said. "Perhaps you'll let me rest here for the matter of a day or so."

He walked behind the bar, where some old blankets were lying, and stretched himself upon them.

"I feel pretty sick. I guess I won't last long. I've got a brother down in the ravine—his name's Driscoll. He don't know I'm here. Can you get him before morning. I'd like to see his face once before I die."

Goskin started up at the mention of the name. He knew Driscoll well.

"He your brother? I'll have him here in half an hour."

As he dashed out into the storm the musician pressed his hand to his side and groaned. Goskin heard the word "Hurry!" and sped down the ravine to Driscoll's cabin. It was quite light in the room when the two men returned. Driscoll was pale as death.

"My God! I hope he's alive! I wronged him when we lived in England, twenty years ago."

They saw the old man had drawn the blankets over his face. The two stood a moment, awed by the thought that he might be dead. Goskin lifted the blanket, and pulled it down astonished. There was no one there!

"Gone!" cried Driscoll, wildly.

"Gone!" echoed Goskin, pulling out his cash-drawer.

"Ten thousand dollars in the sack, and the Lord knows how much loose change in the drawer!"

The next day the boys got out, followed a horse's tracks through the snow, and lost them in the trail leading toward Pioche.

There was a man missing from the camp. It was the three-card-monte man, who used to deny point-blank that he could play the scale. One day they found a wig of white hair, and called to mind when the "stranger" had pushed those locks back when he looked toward the ceiling for inspiration on the night of December 24, 1861.

Preachers and Presents Everywhere
Christmas on the Comstock

In 1859, after they heard about the discovery of gold and silver, men began sweeping into the area on the east slope of Mount Davidson, twenty-four miles southeast of what is Reno today. This place at about 6,220 feet is where Nevada began, later becoming a state in 1864.

People moved to the area with high hopes and expectations to strike it rich, and some achieved their goal. The rush created Virginia City, a cultured town, where the people celebrated the yuletide as they had when they were children. The mining area underneath this exciting town became known as the Comstock Lode.

A city sprang up almost overnight, as wives and children soon followed the prospectors into the area. Next, businessmen came to open stores, lodging houses, theaters, and retail and mining establishments to supply the needs and desires of the fortune hunters and their families. These pioneers built wooden structures along the four or five dirt roads carved into the side of Mount Davidson.

This Christmas story is about celebrating the holiday in a cosmopolitan city, not a crude mining camp. The Virginia City residents lived in a stylish city with a variety of amenities that were found in other major cities, such as San Francisco.

In December 1863 more than four thousand residents of Virginia City in the Nevada Territory celebrated Christmas. Like everyone else in the country, they shopped for presents, attended church services, held festive dinners and dances, and enjoyed other types of holiday entertainment.

Many settlers and the newspaper editor remembered their earlier Christmases. On Christmas Eve in 1863, the *Virginia Evening Bulletin* published an editorial on the meaning of Christmas. The editor bemoaned that the holiday had become more about the worshiping of the dollar than the remembrance of Christ's birth. The newspaper also urged readers to remember the courageous soldiers in cold bivouacs risking their lives to defend the country in the Civil War.

Two days before Christmas, men and women bundled up against the biting cold air walked along C Street (the main street) and stopped in amazement as butcher John Korner cleverly advertised his Christmas turkeys for sale. He herded a squawking flock of 184 gobblers along the frozen dirt street to his shop. Those who could afford the plump, tender-looking birds descended on his store to select a turkey to roast for their Christmas feast.

Meanwhile, the ladies and gents bustled up and down the boardwalks to window-shop and buy presents. In this cosmopolitan town, the customers selected Christmas gifts from a wide variety of merchants. A major store, S. Wasserman & Co. Emporium, in the International Hotel, sold fancy gifts. These included everything from fine china and silver-plated ware to French and Bohemian glassware, Italian vases, Japanese goods, white marble statuettes, charming paintings and engravings, photograph albums, and toys. The customers found that the store also regularly stocked a fine selection of cigars, tobacco, Meerschaum and other fancy pipes, stationery, playing cards, and musical instruments.

At Sam Rosener's store on C Street, the gentleman searching for the perfect gift for the special woman in his life found such items as tortoise-shell jewelry boxes and combs. Looking for intellectual presents, the patrons of Bernhard Franz's Book and Music Store discovered a selection of not only books but also opera glasses, frilly fans, elaborate scrapbooks, ladies' traveling satchels, diaries, almanacs, and 1864 calendars not only in English, but also in French, German, and Spanish. Women searching for materials for new clothing looked over and stroked a wide selection of black and plain-colored silk, French poplins, wool plaids, and Empress (wool) cloth at N. Myers's shop on North B Street.

In 1863 shopping did not end on Christmas Eve. The stores remained open on Christmas Day, and the newspaper reported that lighthearted parents spent lavishly on gifts for their sons and daughters at Fred Dale's store. Born in England, he possessed the right connections to successfully import fancy goods and toys to the delight of the local children and their parents. That year the residents' choices for gifts in Virginia City rivaled those sold in San Francisco shops.

In addition to buying and giving presents, the residents attended church services to observe the holiday. Seven congregations built churches or found places to meet and hired pastors to offer Christmas and other services. The Catholics attended either one of the masses offered by Father Patrick Manogue (later bishop of Nevada) at St. Mary's in the Mountains Church or services at the church recently opened by the Passionist fathers, located between Virginia City and Gold Hill. The Protestants decided between two Episcopal churches, two Presbyterian churches, and the Methodist Episcopal Church for their place to worship.

Besides services, the excited Sunday-school scholars of the Methodist Episcopal Church and St. Paul's Episcopal Church entertained their parents and friends with performances on Christmas Eve. Rev. C. V. Anthony, the pastor of the Methodist church, supervised the children's pageant and services at his elegant church on the corner of D and Taylor Streets.

At St. Paul's Episcopal Church, the Sunday-school children sang several carols in the festively decorated thirty-four-by-sixty-foot Gothic church on the corner of F and Taylor Streets. Rector Franklin Rising installed a stately Christmas tree in front of the altar and lit the evergreen with three hundred wax tapers. The pine scent filled the church as he hung little keepsakes for the scholars on the evergreen tree's branches. He and his congregation decorated the rest of the church with pine boughs, an angel figurine, the red and white Crusaders battle flag, and the red, white, and blue American flag. Rising briefly addressed the youngsters, and then, to close the evening's entertainment, he called on Rev. Ozi Whitaker, the rector of St. John's Episcopal Church in Gold Hill (later the Episcopal bishop of Nevada), to give a Christmas message to the attentive little ones in church.

Without a church building in Virginia City, D. H. Palmer of the First Presbyterian Church offered services in the two-story Odd Fellows Hall that the Storey County commissioners leased for offices and a courtroom. W. W. Macomber, pastor of the Gold Hill Presbyterian Church, called his congregation together in the Gold Hill Odd Fellows Hall, a few miles down the mountain from Virginia City.

For people without a family or home, the owner of Cowles Restaurant hoped to remind his guests of happier days elsewhere. With that in mind, the restaurateur dished up a choice of delicious-smelling and perfectly browned turkey, goose, duck, and other game and offered other delicacies of the season for his customers' Christmas dinners.

Other businesses also spread the holiday spirit. Grocer and city trustee Louis Feusier and general merchandise-store owner A. S. Tobias generously remembered the inmates in jail. These C Street store owners served the prisoners a sumptuous Christmas dinner.

All in all, the residents of Virginia City celebrated Christmas as merrily as they had when they were children in places far from the Nevada Territory.

Mark Twain's Mentor in Virginia City
Comedian Artemus Ward's Christmas Performances

The following story is about how legendary entertainer and writer Artemus Ward became friends with Mark Twain during Christmas week in Virginia City in 1863.

In the summer of 1863, the "Napoleon of the stage" Tom Maguire recognized the mining boom in Virginia City as an opportunity to expand his successful chain of California theaters into Nevada. The Irishman spent twenty-seven thousand dollars to construct a sixteen-hundred-seat wooden playhouse on a narrow lot along Union Street from D to E Streets. Maguire booked nationally renowned actors and actresses, singers, the most popular of lecturers, and other types of performers in his newly opened theater. Over Christmas week in 1863, Maguire booked the popular lecturer and famous comedian Charles Farrar Browne in Virginia City to play the character Artemus Ward, whom Browne conceived of as an ignorant, illiterate, and inept traveling man.

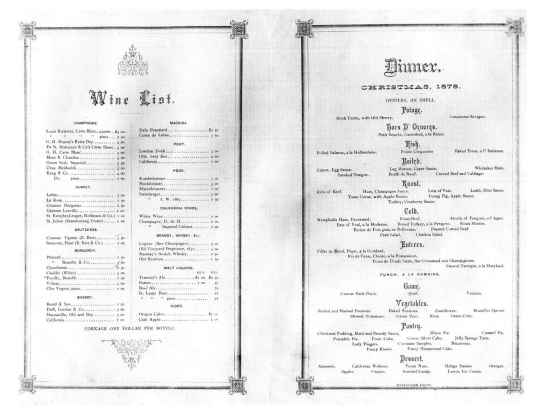

The International Hotel in Virginia City, Storey County, Christmas menu, 1878. This menu shows how sophisticated the town was during its heyday. The hotel building where Artemus Ward and Mark Twain dined was destroyed in the great fire of 1875. The next year a more opulent hotel was built on the same location on C Street, the main street in Virginia City. Courtesy of the Nevada Historical Society.

Before his stage career, the tall, blond-haired Ward had worked as a newspaper reporter and columnist. The copyright laws at the time failed to protect his witty writing, so other newspapers frequently republished his materials without compensating him. Frustrated with being plagiarized and desiring to be paid, he joined the lecture circuit, where his clever words could not be stolen or used for free.

Two days before Christmas, about a thousand people bought tickets to watch Ward's performance in Maguire's elegant theater with its carpeted aisles, oil-burning crystal chandeliers, and soft velvet railings. The audience rocked with laughter and hooted at his antics in the yarn "The Babes in the Woods," about unsuspecting folks who are easily fooled.

Famous for his puns and malapropisms, Ward delivered his funniest lines with a straight face, appearing to be amazed when his audience chuckled.

During Ward's stay in Virginia City, some of the important businessmen in town organized a special dinner at the International Hotel in his honor. The hosts arranged for Ward and Samuel Clemens, a reporter from the *Territorial Enterprise,* better known by his pen name, Mark Twain, to sit together at the table. Because of their shared newspaper experiences, writing styles, and sense of humor, during this meal they developed an immediate friendship. Some believe that Ward inspired Twain to join the lecture circuit and encouraged him to continue writing his amusing stories. When Ward was not onstage, he often hiked up Union Street to the newspaper offices on C Street to chat and trade jokes with Twain.

Ward's engagement with Maguire ended before New Year's Eve. He bid his newly acquired friend Twain good-bye and rode east for his next performance in Austin, Nevada. In 1864 Twain also left Virginia City and became a prolific writer and popular lecturer. Whereas Ward never returned to Nevada, Twain revisited Virginia City to lecture in 1866 and 1868. Twain and Ward corresponded until Ward's death in 1867.

O Tannenbaum! O Tannenbaum!
Reno's Famous and Infamous Christmas Trees

Reno's community tree, a simple pine tree, has always been popular with residents. Renoites first displayed a community tree at East First and North Virginia Streets on the north side of the Truckee River in the 1860s. Since then, as if it were a traveling circus tent, the city employees have repeatedly pulled up the tree's stakes at one site, moved to another place in town, and pounded the stakes in to erect a new community tree. Finally, in 2006, the tree's place of honor came full circle back to the corner of East First and North Virginia Streets.

This history recounts the tree's locations, mentions the prominent residents associated with it, and describes how it became famous when it received national media attention.

Reno's postmaster in the late nineteenth century Samuel Jamison recalled the city's first fragrant pine tree displayed on Christmas Eve in 1868 or 1869. Jamison, his wife, Amelia, and their children, as well as many other families, enjoyed the magic of Christmas as it unfolded around the tree inside Alhambra Hall, located on the southeastern corner of Front (now East First) and North Virginia Streets.

In 1916 the tree moved to a new location on the Carnegie Library grounds at Mill and South Virginia Streets, across from the Riverside Hotel. Baptist minister Brewster Adams suggested that the town erect the community tree outside. Adams anticipated that in its outdoor location, the tree would attract the attention of eastern newspapers. This attention would, in turn, attract thousands of people to visit Reno, who would then visit the many businesses and, perhaps, settle in the town. In this way, the outdoor tree would not only be of sentimental value to the current residents of Reno, but also aid in the further growth of the town.

The manager of the Verdi Lumber Company, Chester Bridgeman, assisted with the tree-erecting project. On December 20 Bridgeman and his assistant found a stately fir in the mountains near Verdi. Chopping down the tree left both men so exhausted and sore that they took the next day off from work. After the tree arrived in town, experienced telephone company linemen erected the evergreen at its new location. Strong winds challenged even these experienced workers, and they had to use three steel guy wires to keep the tree upright.

City electrician Louis Seitz spent two days stringing six hundred colored lightbulbs on the tall tree. At the top he placed a mammoth star controlled by a "flasher" that systematically changed the colors of the lights. The star's message was "Peace on Earth, Good Will Toward Men." This common holiday sentiment took on added meaning at this particular time, as World War I was raging in Europe.

During the evening of December 22, snow quietly fell on downtown Reno, covering the colorfully lighted tree and the ground. The snow

The Reno Arch in 1938. The original arch was built in 1926 to celebrate the Transcontinental Highway Exposition. The town's slogan, "The Biggest Little City in the World," was added to the arch in 1929. Courtesy of Jerry Fenwick.

fulfilled the residents' dreams of a white Christmas. Yet, sadly, the beautiful scene did not draw the national media attention that Brewster Adams desired. Nonetheless, the residents of Reno were still able to enjoy the beautiful outdoor tree.

By 1920 World War I had ended, and the tree took on a new role. During that year the US government launched a national effort to raise money for food and medical services for the three million starving children in Eastern and Central Europe who had been left devastated by the war.

In Washoe County businesses, churches, local lodges, labor unions, and women's organizations participated in this effort through a program called "Buy a (Christmas Tree) Light, Save a Life." Residents were encouraged to purchase a colored lightbulb for $10 (about $113.33 in 2012 dollars) that would then be hung on the thirty-foot community Christmas tree. A symbol of life, each light represented a child saved.

On the cold but clear Christmas Eve the town staged a spectacular program to culminate the fund-raising efforts. By now the tree had moved yet again, to the lawn of the Washoe County Courthouse on South Virginia Street. Bright searchlights in Powning's Park across the street from the courthouse provided illumination, so that the three thousand attendees could see the enormous tree and watch the pageant.

The tree-lighting ceremony included entertainment, music, and a speech from attorney and former Nevada Supreme Court justice Frank Norcross. With his political and legal experience, Norcross delivered a persuasive message about the importance of contributing to the town's efforts. "Remember that Christmastime should come to all the children," Norcross implored the gathering, both "at home and abroad." After his speech even more money was raised, with many a $5 and $10 bill added to a collection plate circulating through the crowd. When the fund-raising campaign ended after Christmas, the relief committee collected more than $2,000, a generous contribution to feed the hungry children.

In 1925 the tree moved again, this time to Wingfield Park. That year Mayor Edwin Roberts thought a lighted municipal tree would add to the festive mood in town. He accepted drugstore owner William Cann's donation of a fifty- to sixty-foot fir tree that was growing in Cann's yard on Jones Street. On December 16 a city crew dug up the tree, trucked it to the east end of the Wingfield Park island, and replanted the tree.

On December 22 the city electrician climbed to the top of the tree and began to hang colored lights on its branches. The tree was so large that it took two days to completely hang them all. The time and effort were well spent, however, for on Christmas Eve hundreds of people gathered in the park to watch as Mayor Roberts presided over the official lighting of the tree.

The city kept its community tree tradition in Wingfield Park until 1999. In that year the city decided to erect and decorate a stately tree across the north channel of the Truckee River in the West Street Plaza Park. In 2006 the city once again moved the site of Reno's majestic evergreen tree to outside city hall, in the plaza along the Truckee River on the corner of East First and North Virginia Streets. This was the same site where the original community tree stood in the late nineteenth century. Unlike Reno's original small indoor Christmas tree, though, the trees in the 2000s were gigantic and erected outdoors in the plaza.

In 2009 the city lit the tall evergreen tree and hung on its branches large holiday ornaments that included gingerbread men, nutcrackers, and multiple large red bows. At the top of the tree was a white star. Passersby strolled downtown to the sounds of joyful Christmas music floating in the air, broadcast from hidden speakers along the street.

The next year, just as Brewster Adams predicted in 1916, Reno's municipal tree made the national news and drew attention to the city. The tree publicity was not exactly beneficial; Reno's tree was newsworthy because it was crooked.

Waltzing Through the Sagebrush
Victorian Christmases in Humboldt County

The original seat of Humboldt County from 1861 to 1873 was called Unionville. It was given this name in 1861, when local miners changed it from Dixie to Unionville in allegiance with the Union during the Civil War. The modest town comprised several hundred wooden shacks and cabins built high up in a narrow canyon on the eastern slope of the West Humboldt Range in north-central Nevada. Today, only a few buildings remain on either side of the one-lane road up the gully.

In 1868 northeast of Unionville, the Central Pacific Railroad laid its tracks through what is now the Winnemucca area and built a train depot. Named after a local Paiute chief, Winnemucca is located on what is now Interstate 80 alongside the Humboldt River. As more people settled there, the city's population outpaced Unionville's. In 1873 the legislature voted to move the Humboldt County seat from Unionville to Winnemucca.

The following stories detail some of the interesting Christmas traditions observed by the residents of Humboldt County during the Victorian Era.

In Victorian England grand balls (dances) and dinner parties were popular Christmastime celebrations. These festive traditions were imported to America throughout the nineteenth century, and they were the entertainment of choice in most Nevada mining camps, especially in Humboldt County. In 1869 two dances and dinner parties competed for attendance from the large population of Unionville. One was held in Cavin's Hall and the other in the Exchange Hotel, and for both the party promoters charged five dollars for their event. Eventually, as mining declined in the area and the population shifted to the northeast, new parties that rivaled those of Unionville's glory days were thrown in other places in the county.

One of these was held in Winnemucca on December 23, 1870, when the widow Margaret Ragsdale sponsored a Christmas ball at her spacious Magnolia Hotel. To guarantee a full house and large crowd, she wisely invited people from not only Winnemucca, but throughout Humboldt County. These included the railroad towns of Battle Mountain, Carlin, Golconda, and Mill City (all these places are now located along Interstate 80); the mining camps of Unionville and Star City; and the ranching communities of Dun Glen and Paradise Valley. No matter from how far away, a good many of those invited made the journey to attend the grand ball at the Magnolia Hotel.

The travelers no doubt felt that their journeys were worthwhile. Claiming her hotel table was the best this side of Sacramento, Ragsdale served them a superb banquet. She employed a Chinese chef to cook all the delicacies she had purchased from the California markets. These included fish and oysters, chicken and other tender meats, and green vegetables. She offered the diners a choice of coffee or tea with their meal. And, of course, if liquor and cigars were desired, Ragsdale promised that no matter the brand, it was available from the barkeep in the hotel bar.

Two decades after the grand party at the Magnolia Hotel, on Christmas Eve in 1890, another splendid Christmas gathering was held in Winnemucca at the Italianate brick courthouse. This time the guests, including children, were treated to a visit from Santa Claus. As the families arrived for the party, they heard the band playing Christmas selections. The little tykes and their parents smelled the scent of the pungent pine tree before they crowded into the district courtroom. As the children entered the room, their eyes shone in anticipation when they spied the magnificent Christmas tree and several tables loaded with presents.

When Santa Claus appeared, the boys and girls were thrilled and were even more excited to receive a gift from him. As they left the party, many attendees were overheard saying that the evening was an absolute success and reflected favorably on the ladies, who planned the party.

That same year promoter Andrew Erickson arranged a ball on Christmas night in Unionville. He hired to play lively dance music a local miner, John Thornton. Thornton strummed his banjo, and the ladies and gentlemen waltzed around the floor, dressed in their finest holiday clothes. Before the dance twenty-year-old Ellen Springer arranged a sumptuous feast at her parents' house in the Upper Town of Unionville. Springer prepared dishes that were fit for the "queen's own taste," and all the diners enjoyed the hearty meal.

The next Christmas, in 1891, in Golconda, a railroad stop seventeen miles east of Winnemucca, the residents donated sixty-six dollars for the town's Christmas celebration. The group obtained a fresh evergreen tree and completely covered it with sparkly ornaments and placed colorfully wrapped presents underneath. When people first smelled and saw the beautiful tree, they nodded in agreement that it was the best they had ever seen in town. Near the tree the schoolchildren sang Christmas songs and recited yuletide selections before their smiling family members and neighbors. The crowd roundly applauded each perfectly delivered dialogue and recitation.

Then Santa Claus arrived to distribute the gifts from under the tree to everyone in town. The planning committee played a little joke on old Santa and startled him as he handed out gifts. Mrs. Claus in her bright-red dress swished into the room, much to Santa's surprise. He was not expecting her, but he enjoyed the prank and recovered his wits before the party ended. At a late hour everyone went home with stuffed pockets and arms full of presents. As they said good-bye, many in town wished Christmas came every week.

This 1891 event concluded another successful round of Victorian dances and holiday parties in Humboldt County, a tradition begun in

Unionville in the 1860s. The residents journeyed not over the river and through the woods, but through the sandy valleys and greenish gray sagebrush for long distances to celebrate their favorite Victorian Christmas traditions.

Reno Churches Competed for Attendance
Trees and Santa Were the Enticements

The Central Pacific Railroad selected Lake's Crossing in the Truckee Meadows to build a depot, laid out the Reno town site, and then auctioned off lots in 1868. Even though Nevada is not known for dense forests or abundant evergreen trees, Renoites maintained their customs of decorating fir trees and inviting Santa Claus to their churches. During the yuletide season, the church members rode, hiked, or drove wagons into the Sierra Nevada to harvest Christmas trees. The town folk found bushy piñon and juniper trees scattered throughout the nearby mountains. The trees were difficult to cut because of their sharp needles covered with pitch as sticky as honey.

This story is about the early Reno churches and the efforts the different congregations made to attract people to their churches, hoping to add new members through their joyful doings.

Every December Reno congregations sought to draw people to their churches by offering Christmastime activities. In 1871 Pastor R. A. Ricker of the First United Methodist Church invited everyone in Reno to his large church, the first church building in town, on the corner of West First and North Sierra Streets, for its Sabbath school's concert on the evening of December 23. The residents smelled the fragrant Christmas tree as they packed the church that night. The program consisted of festive songs and well-delivered recitations, and the highlight of the night was the reading of the "Christians' Christmas Tree." Following the program Santa Claus's appearance delighted young and old, and he distributed the presents hanging on the colorfully adorned tree to little ones so excited they shivered with excitement.

In 1874 the ladies of the Methodist congregation added hearty banquets to their holiday activities. On Christmas Day the church women rolled up their sleeves and cooked a free meal that they served to congregants and other hungry Renoites. To pay for the free meals and to help furnish their church, that evening the tireless women cooked and sold oysters. The following Christmas the church's new minister, Rev. G. W. Fitch, arranged an unusual display: a log cabin filled with goodies. There is little doubt that these fun programs, free meals, and unique displays during Christmastime attracted new members to the First United Methodist Church.

Similar to the Methodists, the congregation of Trinity Episcopal Church sought to attract new members during Christmastime. Unlike the Methodists, though, the Episcopalians had yet to build a church, meeting instead in the Washoe County Courthouse. Perhaps for this reason William Lucas, who was installed as rector in 1873, decided to attract potential new members to the Christmas service not only with a colorfully festooned evergreen tree, but also with the announcement that no collection would be taken. Rector Lucas apparently decided that to build a church, it was first necessary to grow the congregation and then fill the collection plate.

Several years later the Episcopalians were finally able to build their church. On Christmas Eve in 1879, proud of their new building, they displayed an evergreen cross in the chancel, near the altar, and covered three trees with cornucopias, other ornaments, and presents for each Sunday-school student. Surrounded by this lovely display, Rector William Jenvey told the story "The Tramp's Christmas," a sermon about a boy from New England who falls in love and ventures West but returns home, like the prodigal son, to marry his childhood darling. Of course, they live happily ever after. One cannot help but wonder if the good rector was subtly warning congregants that they should not stray and join another church.

During the same years the parishioners of the First Congregational Church of Reno sought to increase attendance by adorning their house of worship with two Christmas trees, another incentive to attract families. The congregation asked Renoites to purchase enough presents to hang on both of these trees. The residents dutifully shopped along dusty Commercial Row and Virginia Street, where the merchants offered a wide variety of toys, games, candy, confectioneries, and children's clothing. They then left their presents at the church in the afternoon for distribution on Christmas Eve. The residents knew that one tree and its presents were meant for the little folks currently in the congregation, while the other was for the friends whom these young members would hopefully bring to the church.

In 1875 the pastor of the Congregational Church, W. J. Clark, presided over a happy evening with the children singing carols in their high-pitched voices and Santa distributing gifts to those in church. At the end of the evening, some of the boys and girls were overheard saying, "It's a shame that Christmas comes but once a year," because the holiday passed far too quickly. No doubt because of the opportunities Christmastime provided to attract new members, the pastor felt the same way.

As Reno's population grew, the religious denominations continued to (and still do) decorate their churches at Christmastime and welcome visitors, but they no longer feel the need to attract new members through such holiday activities.

The "Nevergreen" Trees
Tonopah's Quirky Christmas Decorations

In 1900 prospector Jim Butler discovered silver and gold in the area of Nye County that would soon develop into the boomtown of Tonopah. Because of the region's arid location in west-central Nevada, vegetation is scarce and pine trees do not grow there.

This is an account of two rather odd Christmas trees that local clubmen fashioned for their Christmas parties in the early 1900s.

On the wall of the Mizpah Club in Tonopah hung a photo titled *The Nevergreen Tree, Tonopah's First Christmas Tree, 1901*. Mrs. Hugh (Marjorie) Brown, wife of the club's founder, recalled seeing it one Fourth of July, the only day of the year when women were allowed into the exclusive men's clubhouse. The "tree" in the photograph was indeed far from the deep green of a normal Christmas tree. To build it the men had cut narrow strips of tan wood from packing crates and hammered them to the sides of an upright two-by-four. For decorations, they dangled red-coated, mild-smelling Edam cheeses from each limb. Although Mrs. Brown thought that the makeshift tree in the picture was pathetic, apparently the club members saw it as a reminder of their childhood Christmases and likely a symbol of their ingenuity.

Such cleverness was not reserved only for the members of the Mizpah Club, though. In 1904 when most of the families in town had resigned themselves to celebrating Christmas without a pine tree, the gentlemen

Tonopah's "nevergreen tree." Because fir trees were nonexistent in the area, the members of the Mizpah Club built this tree to celebrate Christmas in 1901. Courtesy of the Nevada Historical Society.

of the Tonopah Club had other ideas and created another odd evergreen effigy. Believing a Christmas tree vital to their festivities, they erected a large pole in the center of the club room. They then nailed boards to the pole for "branches" and tacked gray-green sagebrush to them for foliage. Last, the men hung small gifts from the shaggy limbs for all the members. Their creation made for a dry and woeful-looking Christmas tree and filled the club room with the reek of dusty outdoors, not the sweet smell of pine. Still, although some considered the strange concoction a holiday dud, others decided to see it as a festive success and danced around it like they would the most beautiful and greenest of Christmas trees.

For entertainment the men of the Tonopah Club arranged for a show that was equally as quirky as their "tree." They asked the lovely Marjorie Brown to sing a solo, and for her accompaniment they secured a talented guitarist named Will Towne. A geologist and field engineer, Towne suggested that before the party he should return home to change out of his dirty work clothes. The clubmen, however, were eager to begin their jolly celebration and insisted that he come straight to the club room after his work shift ended. Thus, when the show began Brown appeared radiant in a filmy white organdy gown with a deep-red silk rose tucked behind one ear in her dark hair. Towne, meanwhile, appeared disheveled in dusty khaki work pants, wool shirt, and boots.

But the men of the club did not seem bothered by the incongruity of the duo. Before a delighted audience, Towne stuck his booted foot on a chair, rested his guitar on his knee, and strummed, while he and Brown sang the many verses of a song called "Mandalay." Although it was plaintive and nostalgic, the song, combined with the strange tree, lifted the mood of the gathering and managed to lessen some of their forlorn feelings in the sandy mining town.

These "nevergreen" trees demonstrate the spirit of resilience and ingenuity among the people who lived in the early mining camps of Nevada, such as Tonopah. This spirit still lives within the people of this state.

Sleigh Tracks in Silver Peak
Alice's Proof of Santa's Visit

John and Alice Harrington moved with their children to the Silver Peak mining camp in Esmeralda County in southwestern Nevada in 1905. John found work there as an engineer in the pumping station at the Pittsburgh Silver Peak Gold Mining Company, one of the larger mining companies that extracted silver in the area. After the mine closed in 1915, the family left town and moved to Reno the next year. Today, lithium is the metal actively mined in Silver Peak.

The following story is based on one of the children's journals. In it Alice Harrington Fuetsch describes the challenges and surprises of her childhood Christmases in a remote Nevada mining camp.

To be ready for Christmas in Silver Peak, Alice's mother began preparing food around Thanksgiving. Cooking anything became a trial because the closest market was three miles from their house. She started making mincemeat in November, and after she prepared a batch she stored it in the cellar in a large crock covered with brandy-soaked cloths to preserve the food.

The mincemeat and other unique foods were just one way that Alice's mother ensured that the Christmas holidays were memorable for her children. To make sure they received special gifts for the holiday, she ordered all their toys and clothes from a catalog from a California store, to be delivered in the mail. She even managed to keep the gifts a secret, so that the children were surprised on Christmas morning. Happily, each child received one gift they treasured.

A tall rock fireplace stood at the end of their living room, convenient for Santa's arrival and departure. After opening their gifts, little Alice ran outside to look for evidence of Santa's visit. She recalled that each year, she knew that Santa had really been to their house because she saw Santa's sleigh tracks in the snow by the chimney.

PHOTOGRAPHS

EARLY 1900S

Ruth Hilts's watercolor of the Gold Hill Hotel in Storey County. One of the oldest hotels in Nevada, the hotel opened in 1859, according to some, but the government records reflect the hostelry opened in 1861 under the name of the Riesen House. Courtesy of Ruth Hilts.

The Hotel Golden Grill in Reno in 1906. The Christmas tree decorated with goodies was cut by three miners in Chlorine, a mining camp in northwestern Nye County, and transported to Reno. Governor John Sparks is seated on the right in front of the tree and crowd. The governor was the first to receive a gift from the tree, a shiny red apple. Courtesy of the Nevada Historical Society.

A Tonopah saloon decorated with what appear to be sagebrush garlands and crepe-paper bells for the holidays. The men are standing around a roulette wheel and along the bar, ca. 1903 to 1909. E. W. Smith Tonopah Studio photograph. Courtesy of the Nevada Historical Society.

FACING PAGE:

Top: Three children with their piñon pine tree in Tonopah, Nye County, ca. 1909. Some of their gifts include a train, baby-doll buggy, teddy bear, horse-drawn fire engine, tea set, and rocking horse. E. W. Smith Tonopah Studio photograph. Courtesy of the Nevada Historical Society.

Bottom: The Tonopah and Goldfield Meat Company store decorated with streamers and Christmas bells with nine butchers and clerks in Tonopah, Nye County, ca. 1907. Courtesy of the Nevada Historical Society.

A Tonopah banquet with a small Christmas tree on the right end of the table. A Chinese woman stands in the center, and the fourth man from the left is holding a large feathered bird, ca. 1910. Courtesy of the Nevada Historical Society.

FACING PAGE:

Top: The Truckee River in Reno, ca. 1910. A William Cann photograph taken from Belle Isle (now Wingfield Park) facing east, with the Riverside Hotel in the background and the original wooden boardwalk along the south bank of the river. Courtesy of Jerry Fenwick.

Bottom: P & B Ready Roofing company sled transporting four workmen on Commercial Row in Reno, ca. 1910. Courtesy of Jerry Fenwick.

Normal school students in front of their Christmas tree in Eureka, ca. 1919. Courtesy of the Nevada Historical Society.

Happy Holidays in Las Vegas
Community Clubs Provide Merry Celebrations

In 1905 Senator William Clark from Montana, the founder of the San Pedro, Los Angeles & Salt Lake Railroad, arranged for a town site to be laid out in conjunction with the railroad property in the area that would soon become Las Vegas. The railroad auctioned off its lots in May 1905; a city sprang up when about three thousand people rushed to the area to bid on the land.

This story is about how the Las Vegas community joined together to celebrate Christmas in the early part of the twentieth century.

In 1905 the Fraternal Order of Eagles, a nonprofit charitable organization, decided that the new residents of Las Vegas needed to hold a community party to celebrate Christmas. The group approached Superintendent Frank Grace of the San Pedro, Los Angeles & Salt Lake Railroad for assistance, and he agreed to donate the use of a large garage on Main Street, north of the Hotel Las Vegas, for the holiday festivities.

The Eagles organized a merry, memorable, and magical event for the children on Christmas Day. The members announced that the number of presents for each child would be limited to two. People were urged to donate gifts before the joyous event, so that no child would be overlooked by Santa Claus.

The club recommended attendees dress warmly on Christmas night because heating the massive garage would be like trying to heat the outdoors. When the boys and girls arrived and spied the lodge's evergreen tree bedecked with colorful candy, fruits, and nuts, they gleefully skipped around the tree's platform in anticipation of Santa Claus's arrival. In addition to the presents and the tree, the grownups and their little ones were entertained by a special holiday program. The local children delighted the audience by singing Christmas carols, playing piano solos, and staging a play entitled *The Snow Man.*

In 1915, inspired by the news of the beautifully decorated Carson City community tree the year before, the members of the Mesquite Club, a ladies civic organization, spearheaded what became an annual tradition of displaying a community Christmas tree in downtown Las Vegas that continues to this day. That first year these smart women reached out to members of the local churches, labor organizations, fraternal societies and auxiliaries, and local civic leaders to help coordinate the Christmas festivities. The group planned not only to offer the residents a jolly time but also to provide food and gifts for the hungry.

They met at the Chamber of Commerce's office and established separate committees for relief, entertainment, the tree, decorations, and candy to handle the necessary arrangements for each assignment. They erected a giant evergreen tree at the corner of First and Fremont Streets

A Christmas tree surrounded with a platform on Fremont Street in Las Vegas, ca. 1916–25. Courtesy of Special Collections, University Libraries, University of Nevada, Las Vegas.

and bedecked the fir tree with electric lights and shiny ornaments. On Christmas Eve about seven o'clock, many families and their friends arrived early to listen to holiday music before the program began.

At the appointed moment, the tree lights blazed on, to the awe of young and old. Then Santa Claus arrived, toting his huge bag of treats. The children's excitement reached a high note when jolly ol' Saint Nick began handing out the gifts. He looked into each child's bright eyes as he handed him or her a box of candy and an apple or orange.

In 1919 the Christmas committee covered an evergreen tree with glowing colored lights and streamers of red, white, and blue to celebrate the end of World War I the year before. They adopted the theme "Peace on Earth: Good Will to Men," an appropriate message at the end of the global conflict. On that balmy night, the grade school boys' band played yuletide music as the crowd gathered. The choir serenaded the audience with Christmas songs. A group of girls sang Christmas carols while the crowd waited for Santa Claus to arrive.

When he appeared he handed the band leader the very first gift from his sack as a token of appreciation for his services. Then when each child met Santa they told him what they wanted for Christmas, and he gave each of them a present. After each youngster received a gift, Santa announced that if anyone knew of a child who could not attend the celebration, he still had treats in his pack, and if they dropped by city hall, they would receive their goody.

The machinists and Elks each donated $20 to the event—the largest donors. The committee raised $211 ($2,769.02 in 2012 dollars) and spent $10 for the tree, $55.85 for treats, $35.50 for relief, $3.10 for decorations, and $1 for the watchman, for a total expenditure of $105.45 ($1,383.85 in 2012 dollars).

Even though the town erected its first Christmas tree in downtown Las Vegas in 1905, the holiday event became an annual one beginning in 1915. Today, the evergreen tree is erected inside the Fremont Street Experience, a pedestrian mall under a ninety-foot canopy downtown. Santa Claus arrives not by sliding down a chimney but by descending on a zip line to join the merry crowd watching from below.

Christmas in a Tomb

Miners Imprisoned for Forty-Five Days

The primary industry in eastern Nevada's White Pine County from the turn of the century until the 1980s was copper mining. One of the main operators in the area in the early twentieth century was the Giroux Consolidated Copper Mines Company, located southwest of Ely.

This account describes an occurrence that diverted the company's attention from mining during the Christmas holidays.

On December 4, 1907, rocks and dirt fell from the sides of the Giroux Consolidated Copper Mines Company's Alpha shaft. The deluge soon created a cave-in that trapped twenty men below the surface. Topside the workers dropped a cage, or elevator, to the fifteen men at the five-hundred-foot level below and pulled them out of danger. Four miners and a pump man, however, remained trapped farther down under thousands of tons of dirt. Eventually, it was learned that two miners, "Slim" Turner and Mike Constanti, had been crushed to death at the lowest level of the mine, while miners Fred McDonald (nineteen) and Arthur Brown (thirty-two) and pump man Abel Bailey (forty-two), who were at higher levels, successfully dodged the falling debris.

As the dirt fell total darkness enveloped the miners, temporarily blinding the men. The debris also filled their noses and mouths, causing them to gag and gasp for air. Despite these difficulties, McDonald and Brown scrambled up the ladder to join Bailey. An experienced miner, he became the informal leader of the three trapped miners.

Soon after the three men were entombed, mine superintendent Knight Clapp talked with Bailey via the mine telephone. Bailey told Clapp that they were safe and requested that he start pumping fresh air down the six-inch pipe so that they could breathe. Bailey joked with Clapp, saying, "I expect time and a half for three shifts a day during the time of my imprisonment." Then, as more rocks settled, the stones crimped the pipe and cut the telephone line and connection. The men communicated by tapping on the pipe until new telephone wires could be threaded down the reopened tube to the men below.

In no immediate danger and with enough fresh air, the men settled into their predicament. Soon food, candles, and even a pack of cards were lowered down the pipe. The men used these things to pass the time, playing cards and reading newspapers, magazines, and books by candle-light. They also exercised by walking up and down the drift, a horizontal passage located off the mine shaft.

Meanwhile, Clapp began the rescue efforts, employing fifty men to dig down into the shaft. Every day the women of nearby Kimberly cooked the trapped men's meals, and McDonald's brother sent the prepared food down the tube, with breakfast at nine and dinner at five. The three min-ers reacted differently to the regular meals: one gained weight, another lost it, and another stayed the same. To accompany the food, the trapped men boiled tea and coffee in a coal oil can over a fire made from wicking and packing materials in candle grease.

By Christmas the rescuers had not yet reached the miners, so the three men ate a traditional holiday dinner lowered through the pipe. On Christmas Day carolers came from Ruth and Kimberly to serenade the miners via the telephone.

In early January 1908, as the rescuers were excavating, the weight of the debris and rubble bent the supply tube, cutting off the miners' air and food again. Fortunately, the pipe was quickly straightened out and the air flow restored.

On January 18 the rescuers dug down to within thirty feet of the men. The rescuers telephoned the miners, telling them to start digging up and to allow the dirt to run into the drift. Elated, the entombed men began at once, but the falling dirt came down faster than they could shovel. The compartments filled with dust, and the men gasped and choked in the stifling mine. Finally, the avalanche of debris stopped. With only one shovel, the miners took turns mucking the material out from above them. Soon, a rescuer's foot slipped through the hole, and the shaft began to open up. The trapped miners climbed four hundred feet up the ladder to get to the next level.

Bailey was the first up, and even though he lost some weight during his confinement, he still weighed more than 200 pounds. Three men were needed to pull and tug him through the hole. Finally freed, he wheezed for twenty minutes before he caught his breath. McDonald came next. With his eyes and mouth filled with dust, he struggled through the opening, his already deformed shoulders and the weight he had gained while confined adding to his difficulties. Last, Brown slithered through the hole without any struggle. He weighed 140 pounds, exactly what he weighed before the mine caved in on them.

From there an engine operator used steel cables to position a large bucket that would be used to hoist each man, one at a time, out of the shaft. When the men got into the bucket, they were securely blindfolded, as their eyes had grown unaccustomed to the bright light of the sun. When they reached the surface, they had been entombed in the mine for forty-five days, thirteen hours, and twenty minutes. Loud applause and happy cheers from two hundred friends and coworkers standing around the collar of the shaft greeted the men. The people in Ely celebrated by ringing bells and firing guns, and many residents turned out to express their feelings of gratefulness.

The men were taken to a cottage at Kimberly to recuperate in three darkened rooms, where their blindfolds were removed. In his room Bailey saw his wife, Blanche, and their two children. Meanwhile, McDonald was permitted to see his brother and a few friends. Because Brown had no relatives in the area, he was permitted to visit with some acquaintances. The miners remained at the cottage until the local doctor decided they could safely venture out in the daylight.

When a representative from the *Ely Weekly Mining Expositor* visited the men, he reported that he expected to see three blindfolded, emaciated, long-bearded, and long-haired miners. Surprised, he instead met three hale, hearty, and jovial men walking around the cabin. They were not blindfolded because only a tiny amount of light peeped through the closed blinds. Brown and McDonald were shaved and dressed in their everyday clothes. Bailey had not yet shaved but would before he had his picture taken with his family.

On January 25 the Elks Club held a banquet in the Royal Café to celebrate the men's rescue from the mine. About seventy members, including many miners and mine officials, were present and spoke about their involvement in the liberation efforts. After the crowd made several toasts to the men and their rescuers, the miners spoke. Bailey described his experiences and feelings about his release and thanked everyone again for their efforts. Brown declined to discuss his mental anxiety underground but assured everyone that he was thankful for their work. McDonald simply thanked everyone.

The party ended at midnight, and everyone sang "Auld Lang Syne." Normally, the singing of this Scottish folk song is reserved for the stroke of midnight on New Year's Eve to celebrate the arrival of the New Year. Yet because Bailey, Brown, and McDonald had missed the official New Year's Eve celebrations, the gathering happily made an exception.

Catholics in the Congregational Church
A Gift in the Spirit of Christmas

Around the turn of the last century, fires destroyed three Roman Catholic church buildings in Reno. The first, located on the southeast corner of Center and Fourth Streets, opened in 1871 and burned down in 1879. The second, built in a Gothic style on the northeast corner of Sixth and Lake Streets, went up in flames in 1905.

This story is about the third church and how the other Reno denominations reached out to the Catholics when a giant inferno at Christmastime in 1909 once again left the parish without a home.

After the second Catholic church burned down, Father Thomas Tubman oversaw the building of a new church located on West Second Street and Chestnut Avenue (now Arlington Avenue). Governor John Sparks, other dignitaries, and thousands of residents watched as Bishop Thomas Grace, from Sacramento, laid the cornerstone of the substantial redbrick and gray granite church. Designed with a combination of classical, baroque, and Renaissance architectural styles, the building's distinguishing features were two tall towers with columns supporting conical roofs. Because the University of Nevada had been teaching students in town for twenty years, the bishop named the new church St. Thomas Aquinas, after the patron saint of universities and scholars. When the church was completed, the bishop dedicated it in 1908.

Sadly, like the first two churches, an inferno destroyed the magnificent St. Thomas Aquinas Church on December 21, 1909. The fire started in the Reno Wheelmen's clubhouse, a large two-story wooden structure on Chestnut Street, next to the church. As the conflagration destroyed the clubhouse, sparks flew to the roof of the church. Once the crackling flames took hold, the roof fell in, destroying the rest of the building, despite the valiant efforts of the entire Reno Fire Department. Only the wall and towers on West Second Street were left standing.

Happily, some of the precious artifacts from the church were saved. Months before, Father Tubman had journeyed to Ireland to visit his family and had left his assistant, Father Byrne, in charge. When the fire alarm rang, Byrne and others raced into the church, coughing and choking on the smoke, and managed to save the chalice, other altar vessels, and a few of the pews. The new four-thousand-dollar pipe organ, however, was another story. Organist and choir director Miss Sunderland had stood by it, apparently believing her mere presence would save it. Eventually, she realized that the musical instrument would be consumed in the blaze and abandoned her post.

Learning of the damage to St. Thomas, Rev. C. L. Means of the Congregational Church on the southwest corner of North Virginia and Fifth Streets offered to share his church building and pipe organ with the Catholics on Christmas Day. Because Roman Catholic policy prohibited its members from attending services in other denominations' churches, Byrne wired Bishop Grace in Sacramento for permission to hold services in the Congregational Church. Grace wired back that Byrne should use his best judgment about holding services in a Protestant church. Byrne did not hesitate; the Catholics used the Congregational Church on Christmas morning at 8:00 A.M. and 10:30 A.M., while the Congregationalists held services at 9:30 A.M. and 11:00 A.M.

Although the twenty members of the choir had prepared for weeks in St. Thomas, they still practiced in the Congregational Church. Means allowed Miss Sunderland to play the pipe organ, while the choir rehearsed their hymns in his church. During their services the Catholics turned the pews around to face the rear of the church and set the altar beneath the rear windows. Thus, the choir stood behind the congregation, like the singers would have in St. Thomas.

Not only did Catholics attend the High Mass, but hundreds of people from other churches flooded into the church to attend services. All the seats in the pews were full, and even the choir platform was crowded. People packed the aisles, and after the church filled up many more people were turned away for lack of room.

On Christmas Day Byrne gave a short address to the congregation and visitors about the loss of his church and the gracious way the churches and citizens of all creeds had assisted the Catholics. He thanked everyone for what they had done for the congregation, especially Means and the other ministers in the city, who had also proposed the use of their

The Truckee River in Reno with skaters on the ice west of Belle Isle (now Wingfield Park), ca. 1919. The towers of the St. Thomas Aquinas Church are in the background, and the first Twentieth Century Club building is the dark building on the right. Courtesy of Jerry Fenwick.

churches. Byrne explained that Means had simply made the first offer. He also thanked the Fraternal Order of Eagles and Elks, who had offered the use of their halls, and the manager of the Grand Theater, who had promptly planned a benefit for St. Thomas. Last, he thanked the press for its publicity on behalf of the parish. Everyone in church praised Means for the generous and thoughtful donation of his church.

When Father Tubman disembarked from Ireland in New York City on Christmas Eve, he received a telegram from Byrne reporting that St. Thomas had been destroyed by fire three days earlier. Tubman rushed as quickly as the trains could take him across the country to Reno to begin the reconstruction process.

With the support of his parishioners and many other residents, Tubman quickly rebuilt St. Thomas, and Bishop Grace consecrated the church before Christmas in 1910. That year the ladies in the congregation decorated the rebuilt church with a large array of colorful flowers, green potted plants, and other seasonal decorations. Tubman presided over the services, and the parishioners listened to the new melodious pipe organ and choir members singing Christmas hymns during the mass. The horrible fire of the previous year began to fade in the Catholics' memories, but they recalled the generosity of the other denominations in their plight—a true gift in the spirit of Christmas.

O Christmas Tree
Nevada's Oldest Growing Community Tree

Unlike most other community Christmas trees that are cut down and erected in Nevada towns, the Carson City tree is a living evergreen growing on the state capitol's grounds. The Renaissance Revival tan-sandstone capitol building opened in 1871, and the legislature voted to improve the land around the structure in 1875. The next year the Nevada Board of Capitol Commissioners contracted with a local farmer, George Washington

Gale Ferris Sr., to plant a garden in the Capitol Square. He purchased 255
trees and shrubs from Galesburg, Illinois, where he lived before moving to
Nevada. After the trees arrived in Carson via the Virginia & Truckee Rail-
road, he planted 60 evergreen trees, 30 sugar maples, and 12 other variet-
ies of trees and shrubs on the capitol grounds.

This story is about one of those evergreen trees, decorated by Nevada
officials and local groups for one hundred years.

The members of the Carson City Leisure Hour Club first dreamed up the idea to festoon a living pine tree to celebrate Christmas in 1914. The group asked other clubs and fraternal organizations to join them in arranging the celebration. The organizations decided that one of the tall, stately pines in the southwest corner of the capitol grounds would be the perfect tree to bedeck. The group solicited money to purchase decorations for the tree and gifts for the little ones in town.

On Christmas Eve as people arrived at the capitol, they heard a brass band playing seasonal songs. After the families encircled the gigantic tree adorned with hundreds of colored electric lightbulbs, the excited children began to sing Christmas carols to the band's music. With snow covering the ground, Santa Claus arrived in a bright-red sleigh drawn by two handsome black horses. The fifteen hundred people present heard him coming because of the horses' collars covered with bells that jingled as they trotted up to the capitol. Then Santa invited everyone inside the warm capitol building, where he and his many elves merrily placed eight hundred bags of sweet candies into the outstretched hands of the waiting youngsters. The committee gave fifty of the leftover bags to the Indian Missionary Society and donated seventy-five dollars to the King's Daughters, a charity apparently created by the local French Canadians.

More than two decades later, the people of Carson City were still decorating the living tree on the capitol grounds. In 1937 the Carson 20-30 Club asked Governor Richard Kirman and other members of the Nevada Board of Control to again authorize the decoration of the stately pine tree on the capitol grounds for the Christmas season. The board adopted the club's idea and voted to pay a local electrician forty-five dollars to install four hundred lights on the huge evergreen tree. The grand Christmas Eve celebration that year included about forty carolers who entertained the crowd gathered around the lit Christmas tree.

A few years later, in 1940, the Carson City Business Men's Association suggested a fun twist to the town's usual Christmas celebration. They purchased numerous evergreen trees to decorate downtown. The city bought metal brackets from the Virginia & Truckee Railroad to "plant" the trees along both sides of Carson Street, the main street in town, while a member of the Board of City Trustees donated silver paint to spray the trees. Acting mayor George Martin issued a proclamation in support of the Christmas tree project that promised enjoyment for residents and visitors alike.

An article in the *Carson City Daily Appeal* suggests that in the same year as these additional decorations, the town also held its standard Christmas party on the capitol lawn around the trimmed living evergreen tree. The newspaper reported on the December 15 Christmas party for the youngsters on the capitol grounds, complete with a visit from Santa Claus. That day the kids flitted and dashed around the lawns in front of the capitol, eagerly waiting for the jolly old elf. He finally arrived to distribute gifts and favors to the children, and afterward he sauntered downtown and admired the silver-sprayed trees, likely noting that the pines looked like long silver ribbons along the edges of the street. He also strolled by the festively decorated store windows filled with luxuries for sale for Christmas.

There was yet another twist to the usual celebration in 1973. This time, however, it was not as fun. Because of the energy crisis, Governor Donal "Mike" O'Callaghan decided that the Christmas tree on the capitol grounds would remain as dark as midnight. He also issued a resolution that exterior holiday lighting displays be kept to a minimum. Yet even after the energy crisis abated in the late 1970s, the tree inexplicably remained in its unadorned state for several years.

Finally, in 1988, Governor Richard Bryan revived the community tradition of decorating the living evergreen tree. Dressed in a heavy overcoat to ward off the frigid night air, he flipped the switch to illuminate 750 colored globes donated by the Chamber of Commerce that adorned the majestic tree. "I wish all Nevadans to have a safe and happy holiday

Greeting card of the Nevada State Capitol in Carson City. Courtesy of the Nevada Historical Society.

season," he exclaimed, ushering in the renewed celebration. With his wife, Bonnie, and son, Richard Jr., at the joyous occasion, Bryan mentioned the importance that this particular tree-lighting ceremony held for his family. After ten years in town, they would soon be leaving for Washington, DC, where he would be seated in the US Senate in January. Thus, Bryan's reinvigoration of this Carson City tradition was bittersweet for him.

Bryan's successor, Governor Bob Miller, continued the tree-lighting ceremony. In 1990, joined by First Lady Sandy Miller and their children, Ross, Corrine, and Megan, he once again turned on the tree lights. Bathed in the holiday colors of the glowing lights, the Grace Bordewich Elementary School Choir entertained the crowd by singing a collection of holiday tunes that included "Hark! The Herald Angels Sing," "Children, Go Where I Send Thee," and "White Christmas." They also sang a Native American folk song called "Huron Carol." Then the shivering crowd joined their voices with the choir's in singing "Rudolph the Red-Nosed Reindeer."

One hundred years after the Leisure Hour Club first decorated one of the living pine trees on the capitol grounds, the tradition continues. George Ferris's evergreen tree planted in 1876 is still adorned with colored lights in early December for the holidays.

The Stovall Kids "Planted" a Forest
Christmas in Goldfield in the 1920s

In 1902 prospectors Harry Stimler and Billy Marsh discovered gold in what became the Goldfield area of Esmeralda County in southwest-central Nevada. By 1910 the amount of valuable ore dwindled, the area began to slowly decline, and the town gradually died, as people left for new jobs. In 1920 Alva Stovall took a storekeeper job with the Tonopah & Goldfield Railroad and moved his wife, Emma, and their children, George and Wanda, to Goldfield. When the Stovalls lived in this mining camp, two more children, Ken and Virginia, were born to the family. Like others before him, when Alva lost his railroad job, the family left Nevada in 1931.

This story is about how the Stovall children entertained themselves and other families at Christmastime in Goldfield.

One of Wanda Stovall's earliest Christmas memories was of a particular evening in the 1920s, when she got in trouble as she readied for the community church's Sunday-school holiday program. Clothed in her finest dress, she danced excitedly around the kitchen, waiting to leave for the festive event. When she accidentally brushed up against her father's freshly polished shoes, black steaks marred her lovely white dress. Exasperated, her mother, Emma, ordered her to "sit on the chair and remain there until we leave."

Wanda's older brother, George, had dressed carefully for his role in the program, wearing his Sunday best of a white shirt, a red bow tie, black woolen knickers, and black socks. Unlike the warmer months, though, the first garment he put on was a pair of long underwear. He certainly needed the extra layer, as he would soon be trudging through the icy snow to the church, anxiously thinking about his pending performance the entire way. Wanda, on the other hand, traveled in a more enjoyable fashion. Because Wanda was still very young, her mother wrapped her and her younger brother, Ken, in blankets for a ride in a sled that her father pulled over the sparkling snow to the church.

Eager children and their happy parents packed the building to watch the holiday program. George had practiced and practiced his recital of a rhyme for the event. Yet despite the time he spent at home memorizing his part, when his turn came, he stood speechless on the stage, staring at the audience. Finally, he cleared his throat and said, "If someone will give me a start, I'll say it." After someone shouted out the first two words, he began his recitation and finished it without a glitch. Not even Santa Claus could have given him a better Christmas gift.

As Wanda and her younger siblings grew older, they also participated in the annual Christmas program. At the end of each performance, Santa Claus burst through the double doors of the hall and rushed to the decorated tree. He quickly distributed to each excited child a stocking full of candies and nuts prepared by Santa's helpers, the Ladies Aid Society.

Scarlet fever spread through town in December 1928, so the church canceled the Christmas program. But fear of the disease could not stop Santa, who was still able to visit the homes of all the children in the camp, recalls Wanda. When he reached the Stovalls' house, Saint Nick not only brought gifts to the Stovall children but also to Wanda's best friend, Jacquelyn Thompson, who was staying with them. Later, Jacquelyn thoughtfully mentioned that Santa looked and sounded a lot like her own father.

As part of their routine holiday customs, the Stovalls put up a Christmas tree in anticipation of Santa's visit. Because no pine trees grew in the surrounding countryside, the fir trees were delivered to the town by train. One year too many trees arrived in Goldfield, and they languished in a boxcar at the Tonopah & Goldfield Railroad freight depot. The railroad planned to toss out the surplus trees. When Wanda heard about the proposal, she hitched the family burros to a wagon, and she and her brothers, George and Ken, hauled about twenty trees to their house on Euclid Street. Digging holes in the vacant lot across the street, they "planted" the evergreen trees. The youngsters played in their magnificent forest until the pine needles began to drop and the trees tilted at peculiar angles.

One Christmas morning Wanda crept downstairs before the others awoke. Shivering in her nightclothes and standing in bare feet on the chilly linoleum, she spotted under the tree a toy telephone for her baby sister, Virginia, and a caterpillar toy for brother Ken. She also saw the gift she absolutely wanted, a *Wizard of Oz* storybook as well as another surprise gift for her, a gold signet ring. When she slipped it on her finger, she found the ring was too big for her at the time. Undiscovered by her parents, she tiptoed back to bed.

When everyone in the family awoke later in the morning, she pretended to be gleeful about her new book and ring, but she regretted her earlier trip to the tree. Peeking had taken all the surprise and pleasure out of Christmas morning.

Josephine and the Scary Santa
A Jarbidge Christmas

People worked together in the early Nevada mining camps to produce memorable Christmases for the children in town. One such mining camp was Jarbidge. Located in northeastern Nevada in Elko County, this remote and desolate mining camp sprang up because of the discovery of gold in 1909, and by 1919 the largest gold-producing mines in Nevada were located in Jarbidge. The town's name came either from the Shoshone word Jahabich, meaning "the devil," or from the word Tswhawbitts, the name of a mythical crater-dwelling giant who roamed the area.

The following account is about how Josephine Cooper and her family celebrated one Christmas in Jarbidge in the early 1920s.

Josephine's father, Bill, found a mining job in Jarbidge in 1921, and he moved there from Idaho with his wife and three children. The Coopers lived in town, renting a small house with a kitchen and two tiny bedrooms. Snow frequently covered the ground of downtown Jarbidge, located high in the mountains, in the winter. Josephine recalled that she never tired of the sled rides down the long, sloped main street that ran through the middle of the mining camp.

Like Bill Cooper, many of the young men in town had moved to Jarbidge for jobs in the mines. In the new, likely still unfamiliar surroundings of northeastern Nevada, they fondly recalled their own happy childhood Christmases spent in their hometowns. Possibly nostalgic for those long-ago days in faraway places, the miners wanted to create the same kind of joy for the children of Jarbidge, and they donated money so that each youngster in the camp could receive a gigantic red stocking for the holiday. The local women made these festive gifts, stuffing them with fruit, nuts, candy, and a present, usually a handmade pair of mittens, a scarf, or a cap.

In addition to the stockings, the people of Jarbidge also organized community festivals to celebrate the Christmas season. Josephine recalls one particular year when the highlight of the festival, at least for her, was a school program that included performances by the local children. Only six at the time, Josephine was scheduled to recite a lovely poem about a little girl thanking Santa Claus for the gift that he had brought her. For such a young girl this was a big assignment, and she painstakingly memorized her lines before the program. Yet no matter how much she had practiced, when the time came she was still nervous. All alone on the stage with knees trembling and tightly clutching her new doll, she drew in a deep breath and bravely recited the poem:

> Just see this lovely dolly that Santa brought to me
> And I'm the happiest girlie that ever you did see.
> If I could see old Santa, I'd give him a great big kiss.

All of a sudden, Santa Claus appeared on the stage. With arms out-stretched, he began walking toward her for the promised kiss. Terrified, Josephine fled the stage in tears.

Perhaps it was for the best that she did not stay for the kiss, though, as she may have discovered a secret that would have ruined her childhood wonderment of the jolly old elf. Years later and long after the family had left Nevada, Josephine learned that her father played Santa Claus that year.

Christmas Comes to Yerington
Plans and Surprises

Lyon County is located in the west-central part of Nevada and contains several communities: Yerington, Smith Valley, Wellington, Mason, Dayton, Fernley, Silver Springs, and Silver City. In some areas of the county, the main industry is agriculture, while in other places the people make their

living from mining or manufacturing or in retail or gaming establish-
ments. The county seat is in the city of Yerington, a town with a vibrant
business community, including two casinos.

Clark Guild, a native of Dayton, was among the most influential men
in Lyon County and the state of Nevada. In 1908 the voters elected him as
auditor-recorder of the county. After Guild joined the Nevada State Bar in
1914, the voters elected him Lyon County district attorney in 1916, a posi-
tion that he held for eight years. He finished his career as a district court
judge, serving from 1925 to 1953. He is known as the "father" of the Nevada
State Museum and cofounder of the Nevada Day celebration. He was also
father to Marjorie Guild Russell, Governor Charles Russell's wife and the
first lady of Nevada from 1951 to 1959.

The following story describes Guild's role in Yerington's Christmas cele-
brations in the 1920s.

Along with his official duties, Clark Guild chaired the Yerington Community Christmas Tree Committee in 1923. Ten days before Christmas, he called to order the planning meeting in the Lyon County Courthouse, located on Main Street. Men and women from every civic and
fraternal organization attended to coordinate the yuletide celebration.
The group voted to tell Santa Claus that he should bring candy, fruit,
nuts, and a present for each child in the town.

Once this official vote was taken, the planning committee separated
into smaller groups, each charged with various tasks to prepare for the
holiday cheer. One group was organized to raise money, another to
obtain two Christmas trees, still another to purchase gifts for the town's
children. The group that was in charge of the Christmas trees erected one
in the middle of Yerington's main street and the other at Rink Hall, the
old skating rink converted into a large meeting hall, located downtown.

Santa Claus must have gotten word of the official vote, because a few
days before Christmas Guild announced that Saint Nick had sent a special message, confirming that he would soon be visiting Yerington. Moreover, he asked that every girl and boy meet him at Rink Hall at exactly
8:00 P.M. on Christmas Eve. The busy elf noted that because he had many
visits to make and a long trip ahead of him, he could not get to Yerington
before then.

The late hour of Santa's meeting time did not deter the people of the town. On Christmas Eve a record-breaking crowd attended the party. While the children waited in the festively decorated and pine-scented hall for Santa's arrival, a saxophone band played several holiday selections and the high school's glee club sang Christmas carols. Then, on the stage near the beautifully trimmed Christmas tree, the schoolchildren presented a skit, *A Visit to Santa Claus,* dressed in costumes for their roles as Mrs. Claus, Jack-in-the-Box, and other holiday characters.

Near the fateful hour of 8:00 P.M., in the middle of the program, Santa surprised everyone when he jumped out of the open fireplace on the stage. He gave each boy a toy horn and each girl a doll, and every child received a big bag of candy. As the boys began to blow their horns, the crowd was soon engulfed in a din that likely sounded joyous to a few and discordant to most. Perhaps this is why the evening program ended shortly after Santa handed out the presents.

Governor Charlie and Marjorie Russell celebrating Christmas in the Governor's Mansion in Carson City. The child reflected in the mirror is their son David, ca. 1951–58. Courtesy of C. David Russell.

The following year Santa provided yet another surprise for the people of Yerington. As the 1924 Christmas party began, the transformer blew in Rink Hall, leaving the auditorium pitch-black. Despite this setback, when the lights came back on, the kids discovered Santa Claus had snuck in. Like his reindeer, he pranced around the Christmas tree, amusing the people in the hall. Santa pulled from his pack two big stockings for each child, one filled with small toys and one overflowing with nuts and candy. The hard work of Clark Guild and the other residents of Yerington had again made the town's Christmas holiday a success. And once more Santa's surprise only enhanced the careful plans.

The Richest Christmas
Snowbound on the Swallow Ranch in 1923

In the first part of the twentieth century, families who lived on ranches isolated far from major Nevada cities in towns sometimes "made do" with available resources to celebrate Christmas. Matilda and Richard Swallow owned one such ranch. About fifty-five miles southeast of Ely in White Pine County in east-central Nevada, the Swallows operated a cattle and sheep ranch large enough to require extra help. When Levi Olds worked as a ranch hand for the Swallow outfit during the 1920s, he brought his wife, Kate, and their children to live on the ranch.

This story is about how one of their children, Sheldon, who was five years old in 1923, experienced the most memorable Christmas of his childhood.

When a blizzard struck a few days before Christmas of 1923, the storm further isolated the Swallow Ranch behind huge snowdrifts, completely cutting off access to the outside world. Because the ranch hands could no longer travel to their own hometowns to visit their extended families for the holidays, Matilda and Richard Swallow invited them to a Christmas Eve party in the big dining room of the bunkhouse. Like Levi Olds, many of the ranch hands brought their immediate families to live on the ranch, and the Swallows also invited the wives and children of these men to the party.

Sheldon Olds remembers that he and his siblings dressed in their best Sunday clothes for the party. Meanwhile, his dad harnessed a team of horses to pull the family in a bobsled from their house to the Swallows' bunkhouse. When the sled arrived, Sheldon and his siblings bravely climbed into the sled, and their mother tightly wrapped them in blankets. The family snuggled together all through their trip to the party.

When they arrived at the bunkhouse they were greeted by a blazing fire in a large fireplace that the Swallows lit to heat the room against the frigid cold. Once settled in, the Olds family joined the other guests in singing holiday songs and carols. They then listened as a small group of cowboys sang American folk songs to guitar accompaniment, including "Oh My Darling, Clementine" and "Turkey in the Straw," followed by a young girl playing Christmas music on her accordion. As the music played, Matilda Swallow and two ranch hands began to carry out large platters stacked with ham and beef sandwiches, cookies, cakes, and pies. She urged everyone to "pile in and eat your fill" and served homemade root beer to wash down the food.

After the meal Sheldon heard the loud clanging of sheep bells in the hall, followed by a hearty "Ho, ho, ho!" He knew it was the sound of Santa, but the jolly old elf who arrived was not dressed like Sheldon expected. Instead, this Santa wore a sheepskin-lined denim jacket and tucked his pant legs into cowboy boots. On his head perched a big woolen stocking with a red ribbon tied around the toe. For a beard he draped a piece of white cloth across the lower part of his face. Yet despite the man's unusual attire, little Sheldon thought he looked like an "honest-to-goodness Santa."

The Saint Nick of Swallow Ranch carried over his shoulder an overflowing gunny sack filled with goodies that he distributed to all the guests. He handed everyone a large round brightly colored object. When Sheldon received the present he had no idea what it was, and as he stood holding his gift he looked up questioningly to his father. "It's an orange, son. It's an orange," explained his father. Sheldon watched others peel and eat their gifts, but he thought the fruit too exquisite to ruin like that. His mother, though, entertained no such reverence and gave him sections of hers.

After Santa finished handing out the oranges, Richard Swallow stood up and conducted a drawing for door prizes. Everyone received a prize. Yet when Sheldon heard his name called, he was surprised because he did not think Mr. Swallow would give him a gift. A month or so before Christmas, Sheldon and his best pal, the Swallows' six-year-old son, Arlo, were naughty. They went into the corrals searching for innocent adventure but instead managed to set fire to and completely burn down a tall stack of straw in the center of the barnyard. Knowing they were in big trouble, the boys ran to the dipping pens and hid in the new sheep wagon. Somehow or another they managed to set that on fire, too. Sheldon remembered the swift and unpleasant punishment when they were discovered. Since then, Sheldon had successfully managed to avoid Mr. Swallow.

As Sheldon walked toward Mr. Swallow to receive his gift, the man seemed like a twelve-foot giant. Sheldon began to worry that rather than a gift, Mr. Swallow planned to give him another unpleasant punishment. Terrified, Sheldon turned to his mother and clung to her. She moved him inch by frightful inch forward and finally shoved him toward the looming Mr. Swallow. The man towered over Sheldon like a huge monster, and the boy trembled as he awaited his fate.

Yet Mr. Swallow did not look angry and instead flashed a broad and merry smile across his face. The man slowly began to search through a pile of gifts on a nearby table. When he pulled out a box wrapped in beautiful paper, Sheldon began to realize that he had been forgiven. Still, when Mr. Swallow tried to hand Sheldon the box, the boy remained too frightened to move. Mr. Swallow lifted one of Sheldon's arms and slipped the box under it. With his new treasure squeezed to his side and clutching his precious smooth orange in the other hand, he started backing away slowly, never taking his eyes off Mr. Swallow. When Sheldon reached the center of the room, he turned and dashed to the safety of his mother's lap. Watching the boy's performance, everyone in the room roared with laughter.

When the party ended Sheldon's mother bundled up the children for their bobsled ride home. Fortunately, before they left the warmth of the bunkhouse, the wind stopped blowing and only a little snow fell softly to the ground. Needing no encouragement and eager to get to the warmth of their stable, the horses raced over the hard-packed snow to the family's cabin.

The family was happy to return to the warm safety of their home. Sitting around the fire, dressed in their nightclothes, they popped the corn they had raised that summer. Sheldon's mother then brought out his gorgeous box. Gently, she removed the wrapping on the box, and the family discovered the most delicious-smelling assortment of store-bought chocolates. His mother asked Sheldon if he would like to share his gift, and he agreed. Almost reverently, his mother lifted each chocolate out of its little brown paper cup and cut it into quarters. She then put the candies on a plate for Sheldon to proudly pass around. They slowly savored the yummy feast, one quarter at a time, making the sweet joy last a little bit longer, truly an extraordinary delicacy for the family. All too soon the chocolates were gone, and the children went to bed. Sheldon tucked his big beautiful orange securely under his pillow before he fell asleep to dream of that unique Christmas Eve.

Because of the snowstorm, "Santa" could not get to the store to buy any presents that year, so there were no gifts to open on Christmas morning when Sheldon awoke. But it did not matter. More than sixty years later, Sheldon remembers this simple Christmas as the richest and most enjoyable one of his childhood.

Churches and Courthouse Trees
Eureka's Holiday Spirit in the 1920s

Prospectors discovered a high quality of silver and lead ore in northeastern Nevada in what is now Eureka County in 1864. On making the find, the miners declared "Eureka!" the Greek word meaning "I have found it." The county seat, the town of Eureka is known as the "friendliest town on the loneliest road in America." The old mining camp and its two-story redbrick Italianate courthouse are located on US 50. Southwest of the highway, the county built a public school in 1923 that closed in 1995 and has since been demolished.

The following is an account of how the people of Eureka joined together to create community-wide Christmas tree celebrations in the 1920s.

In 1924 the Catholic, Episcopal, and Presbyterian churches in Eureka decided to erect one community Christmas tree in the school auditorium, rather than having each congregation display an evergreen tree in their own church. In proposing the community Christmas tree, the churches hoped that everyone would unite to celebrate the holiday. Along with fostering a sense of community among the congregants of the many churches, the ministers viewed the Christmas holiday as a way to connect townspeople with both the past and the future. Christmas "takes a person back to the good old days," observed one reporter from the *Eureka Sentinel*, while at the same time, "It is only fair for this community to preserve this institution and this spirit for the coming generation."

The clergymen formed a committee to arrange to decorate a fir tree and to plan the yuletide program. The group decided that every child attending Sunday school would perform in at least one of the numbers. They invited everyone in town, and 250 people turned out to rejoice over the churches' efforts and their first community tree on Christmas Eve. The scent of the freshly cut pine tree permeated the air, as Diamond Valley contractor and member of the Eureka County School Board William Russell presided over the festivities. The audience watched the Sunday-school scholars from the Catholic, Episcopal, and Presbyterian churches perform onstage in the school gymnasium beginning at 7:30 P.M.

The program included the students singing songs such as "If Old Santa Was Our Pa" and reciting stories such as "The Hole in the Sock." A few children were selected to recite Christmas poems and stories. When the program concluded, Santa Claus swept into the room. As he described the difficulties of his nocturnal trip, his white hair and whiskers gently jiggled as he spoke. Then, with the help of a few high school students, he passed out boxes of candy, nuts, and popcorn balls to the eagerly waiting little ones. After Saint Nicholas personally greeted all the kids, he waved good-bye and flew off to finish visiting the stockings of all the good little girls and boys elsewhere in Nevada.

A *Eureka Sentinel* reporter commended the churches for their cooperative spirit and for setting aside their differences when it came to benefiting the community. He observed the delight and satisfaction of the crowd and believed that everyone thought the event was a great success. The journalist hoped this was the first in a long series of future community celebrations. But in the coming years, the churches returned to their previous separate festivities and programs in their own churches on Christmas Eve.

In 1928, however, residents remembered the merry fun and sense of town unity that resulted from the single community evergreen tree on Christmas Eve. Seeking to reinvigorate this Christmas tradition, they persuaded the county officials to arrange for a community tree in town. This

The Eureka Presbyterian Church. Teachers and Sunday-school scholars celebrating Christmas in the 1920s. Courtesy of the Nevada Historical Society.

time, though, the project was an effort undertaken by the residents, not the churches.

Several men drove into the nearby mountains to search for the perfect community tree. They found what they believed was a good candidate, but after cutting it down and hauling it back to town they decided they could do better, so they returned to the hills. They finally found a ten-foot pine tree near the mouth of Pinto Canyon, southeast of town. They cut it down and trucked it to the sheriff's office for inspection. After careful examination of the pine, the men voted the tree satisfactory and a superb specimen. They adorned the evergreen with yards and yards of gold and silver tinsel, many ornaments, and tiny electric globes. On December 21 they placed this lighted tree on the courthouse balcony, overlooking the main street (Highway 50 today). The officials lit the tree every night until after Christmas.

Unlike the churches' onetime community tree in 1924, the town continues the tradition of displaying a decorated evergreen tree on the courthouse balcony during the Christmas season.

Santa Claus and Yule Missa
Danish and American Christmases

Harold Jacobsen served in several state political offices from the 1940s to the 1980s. Elected to the Nevada Assembly, he represented Humboldt County from 1947 to 1948. He was then elected to the University Board of Regents to represent the fifteen "cow" counties from 1962 to 1974. Finally, the voters elected him the mayor of Carson City, where he served from 1976 to 1984.

His father, Jorgen, emigrated from Denmark to Nevada to join his uncle on a ranch in 1901. After Jorgen married Eureka County native Grace Crofut, they became the parents of six children, with Harold the fourth born. Following his parents' childhood Christmas traditions, Harold and his siblings enjoyed both American and Danish customs.

In the following story Harold Jacobsen describes this mixture of Christmas traditions on his family's ranch in Diamond Valley in Eureka County, Nevada.

Harold Jacobsen remembers a time in 1925, as an eight-year-old, when he and his family lightheartedly hiked up a nearby hill on their Diamond Valley ranch to search for the perfect piñon pine tree to cut down for Christmas. With snow on the ground, they easily slid the six-foot tree down the mountain to their house. His father fashioned a tree stand from the hub of an old freight wagon and set up the tree in a corner of the living room. They never put the tree in water because the piñon pine remained fresh until after Christmas.

The family topped the tree with a star and hung many colored glass ornaments on the branches. They also wrapped the tree with a tinsel garland so long that it circled the tree several times. The kids strung popcorn on a long piece of twine and wrapped it around and around the tree. Harold's older siblings strategically clipped candle holders on the branches, so when the candles were lit, they would not catch the tree on fire. The burning candles enhanced the piñon's piney smell in the house.

"We never doubted that Santa would find our beautiful tree and remember us. We had been good, so Santa would be generous with us," recalls Harold, describing their expectations. As hard as they tried, the kids could never stay awake long enough to catch a glimpse of Santa Claus. On Christmas morning the children found unwrapped presents from the jolly elf under the tree. "We knew whose presents were whose because of what we had asked Santa to bring us," explains Harold. Usually, each child received two to three toys. One year the siblings received a Flexible Flyer. They agreed that the new sled was a vast improvement over the homemade one they had been using.

In addition to the American Christmas traditions, the Jacobsen family also observed Danish holiday customs. On Christmas morning, along with the gifts from Santa, Harold and his siblings would find presents left in wooden shoes. These were left by the Yule Missa (a variation of the Danish Yule Nisse), allegedly a diminutive old man often wearing gray and red wool clothes and a red cap. Like Santa, the Yule Missa also sneaked into the house after the children had gone to sleep. Indeed, no matter how hard Harold and his siblings tried, they never caught sight of this fairy gift giver, either.

Harold's mother also incorporated Danish cuisine into the holidays. She would follow recipes from a cookbook she bought on her honeymoon trip to Denmark. She prepared roast goose and exceptional side dishes, such as raisin soup and rhubarb pudding.

At school, though, the celebrations were those associated with American traditions, not Danish. Harold and his siblings attended a small school a few miles from home, and he recalls performing in its annual Christmas program. His duties included singing carols and reciting Christmas poems. At age ninety-three Harold could still recite the famous story "The Night Before Christmas" word for word without hesitation. And he recalls with fond delight his boyhood Christmases in Diamond Valley, with their mixture of American and Danish holiday traditions.

Santa Claus Rang the Doorbell
Christmas in Lovelock

Born in Lovelock in 1919, Phyllis Anker (later Bendure) grew up on her family's ranch. As an adult she would become an educator, teaching business education to Nevadans in Eureka, Lyon, and Pershing Counties and in Carson City for thirty-four years. Phyllis's grandfather Peter emigrated from Denmark to Nevada in the late nineteenth century, homesteading eight hundred acres about five miles south of Lovelock, the county seat of Pershing County. The town is located on I-80 in the Big Meadows area, near the Humboldt River and Central Pacific Railroad tracks. In 1890 Peter built a large home on the property where he raised his children, including Phyllis's father, Phillip. Her father and mother, Myrtle Talcott Anker, native Nevadans, later lived in the house with their five children.

This story describes Phyllis Anker's Christmas activities on her family's ranch when she was growing up in the 1920s.

At Christmastime the Anker family bought a stately evergreen tree that was so tall it reached the ceiling of their house. Because they had electricity—unusual for a Nevada ranch at the time—they strung electric lights on the evergreen, topped the tree with either an angel or a star, and draped the branches with tinsel. The ornaments they hung on the tree had been handed down or given to them by other family members. As they bedecked the tree, they would say something like, "Oh, this is the ornament Aunt Florence gave us." Each decoration brought back fond memories of the family members, and they reminisced about them as they hung the ornament on the pine tree.

On Christmas Eve the doorbell rang, and their mother announced, "Someone is at the door." The children raced to the door and were astonished to see Santa Claus dressed in his red suit with white trim and black boots standing outside. They invited him in and took turns sitting on his lap. He opened his overflowing black sack and gave them presents of hard candy, fruits, and small inexpensive gifts. His visits lasted for many years, until the children eventually outgrew the custom.

Phyllis later learned that her uncle Barney Wiley played Santa. A few years ago Phyllis rediscovered the suit among her things. The family members restored the white trim on the red suit and cap, freshened up the white beard and mustache, and bought new shiny black boots and glasses. Her son Fred Bendure wore this "new" outfit and appeared at Christmas gatherings to the delight of Phyllis's grandchildren and now great-grandchildren. In a way, then, the same Santa who delighted Phyllis and her brothers and grandchildren also entertained Phyllis's great-grandchildren.

Other yuletide activities Phyllis participated in as a child included a Christmas program at the Grace Methodist Church, located on the corner of Cornell Avenue and Eighth Street. All the kids played a role in the nativity-story performance. Phyllis remembers that "the boys wore bathrobes, appearing as the three wise men, and the other kids dressed in appropriate costumes for their roles." Every child sang a solo, recited a holiday poem, or merrily danced around the stage.

At the Big Meadow School, a two-room schoolhouse, in the larger multipurpose room the students also presented an annual Christmas program. The stage, sophisticated for its time, even had a curtain that opened and closed at the beginning and ending of each performance. Everyone in the Lovelock Valley (about fifty people) showed up for the yuletide program, bringing food to share.

Other wintertime activities that the Anker siblings enjoyed included sledding. Rather than down a hill, though, the sled rides of the Anker children had the unique character of Nevada ranch life. Their old reddish brown horse, "Sally," retired from field work, permitted the children to tie five or six of their homemade sleds into a long line behind her. One of Phyllis's older brothers drove Sally as she patiently pulled them around and around the pasture.

The children were also delighted when the west end of the Humboldt River froze so that they could ice-skate. They held parties on the riverbank and roasted weenies and white marshmallows with their friends and family. These gatherings were all part of the Anker family's winter celebrations. Yet Christmas and meeting Santa Claus were the highlights of the holiday for the Anker children.

"It's a Christmas Tree"
Basque Immigrants and an American Tradition
ROBERT LAXALT

Robert Laxalt came from a prominent Nevada family. His father, Dominique, had immigrated to America from the Basque Country in the French Pyrenees in the early nineteenth century, eventually settling in northern Nevada. Dominique became a successful sheep rancher and married Theresa Alpetche, who was also a Basque immigrant. Four years after Dominique's sheep business faltered, Theresa decided to buy a small hotel in Carson City that they ran as a boardinghouse, primarily for Basque cattlemen and sheepherders. The couple had six children. The eldest, Paul, would enjoy a successful political career that included terms as governor of Nevada and as US senator. Robert became one of Nevada's most prolific and celebrated authors. Among his many books, his best known is Sweet Promised Land, where he recounts his father's return to the Basque Country after living in the United States for almost fifty years.

The following excerpts are from Robert Laxalt's book The Basque Hotel. It tells the story of Pete, the son of a Basque immigrant, and his coming of age in Depression-era Carson City. Pete's immigrant parents run the Basque Hotel, serving sheepherders and town characters. Pete is indifferent to his heritage except for disquiet about his parents' ignorance of American traditions. In the following passages, Pete muses over his relationship with his parents, as well as his childhood memories of Christmas, as he searches on a mountain near Carson City for an evergreen for the family's holiday celebration. He had not told his family of his trip.

. . . It wasn't that the family could not afford to buy a tree or that his father could not go cut one. It was just that neither his father nor his mother seemed to know that a Christmas tree went with Christmas, and the reason was tied up somehow with all the other unexplained things that came out of what they called "the old country."

Pete had considered telling them, but he had not been able to summon up the courage. Whatever way it came out, it would have amounted to a reproach on his part and a failing on theirs. So, there was nothing else to do but keep quiet or tell a lie when his friends who lived in real houses instead of a hotel talked about their Christmas trees. Or worse yet, to have to walk past their homes on the back streets and see the dull glitter of Christmas trees trimmed with tinsel peeping through the windows and feel a pang of loss because Christmas in his family was not complete.

. . . Pete reflected that the business of a tree meant more to him than Santa Claus. He had lost his illusions about Santa Claus at a very early age. It happened one night after the American Legion Christmas party for all the kids in town, when they had trooped up dutifully to accept their presents from that terrifying apparition in a red costume and a long white beard.

When the American Legion party was done, he and his brothers and sisters had gone straight to the kitchen of the little hotel to open their presents. The front door of the hotel burst open and Santa Claus came shuffling down the long dining room jingling the sleigh bells he carried over one shoulder. They had all scurried for cover to their common bedroom and locked the door.

Santa Claus did not pursue them, but they could hear his hearty laugh and the jingling of the bells from the kitchen. Pete had tiptoed to the door and opened it a crack just in time to see Santa Claus hoisting a shot glass of whiskey to his lips. The revelation that Santa Claus drank whiskey did not bother Pete, but the way in which his lips curled around the shot glass did. There was only one man who drank his whiskey that way. The menace of the apparition dissolved and Pete knew that Santa Claus was only the old prospector, Mickey McCluskey, got up in costume.

. . . The wind had died, but it had done its work of bringing in the storm. The air was so filled with huge snowflakes that he could barely make out the evergreens on the white mountain above him. He took a backward look across the fields to town, but the town was no longer to be seen. His chest tightened with a spasm of terror, and he very nearly abandoned his quest. But when he faced the mountain again, the stubborn streak in him took hold. He had come too far to give up now.

. . . There was a Christmas tree to be cut, and in a hurry, before the snow got too deep. It was already around his waist, and the higher he climbed, the deeper it got.

. . . He stared at the tree in despair. All he wanted was to be free of his obligation and go home to warmth. But there was no escaping. He had come too far to go home empty handed. With bitterness in his heart, he picked up the hatchet and plowed his way to the tree and cut it down.

Afterwards, he could not remember much of the long trip home, except that the boughs of the tree on his shoulder kept obscuring his vision and that he fell less often when he had descended from the mountain and gained the even ground of the fields.

He had planned to rest when he reached the safety of the thin line of poplars on the edge of town, but it did not seem worthwhile. By then, he had lost sensation in the hand that held the hatchet, he could not feel the tree trunk biting into his shoulder anymore, and home was only a few blocks away. The lights had come on in the houses on the back streets, and snowflakes played in the glow from the streetlamps overhead. Muffled by closed doors and made soft by falling snow, the high clear voices of children singing carols reached out from a big house.

Main Street was deserted when he reached it. The storm had driven everyone inside. The only lights on his block came from . . . the little hotel. He paused in front of the hotel, trying to straighten himself for the triumphant entry he had daydreamed about sometime in the hazed past. But to straighten up was impossible, so he merely pushed open the door and went inside. Light and warmth and the voices of his sisters, changing in an instant from tears to delight, flooded over him. And then something happened. It was as if the thin wire that had sustained him snapped like a violin string. The tree rolled from his shoulder and the hatchet fell from his hand.

Faces swam into his vision, were transfixed, and then slipped away. He saw his father's face and his eyes wild with worry, . . . the sheriff's fat face in a furry cap and earmuffs and his saying something about a search party, and his mother's face with eyes bigger and darker than he had ever seen and her mouth framing a question.

Pete heard his own voice. It came out in croaking he did not recognize. "It's a Christmas tree."

He tried to take a step. His father caught him when he fell. Pete felt the strong arms close around him and pick him up like a child. And because nothing further was required on his part, Pete leaned his face against his father's chest and went to sleep.

PHOTOGRAPHS

1920S – 1930S

A family with a Christmas tree in Ludwig, a mining camp in Lyon County. Children's gifts include a baby-doll buggy, tea set, book, and horse-drawn fire engine, ca. 1922. Courtesy of the Nevada Historical Society.

A mother and daughter with a piñon pine tree in Thompson, a station on the branch line of the Nevada Copper Belt Railroad, in Lyon County, ca. 1922. Courtesy of the Nevada Historical Society.

The Goldfield Hotel lobby, ca. 1926. The Christmas decorations included a bedecked piñon pine tree and crepe-paper streamers. This hotel opened in Goldfield in 1908 and closed in 1945. Courtesy of the Nevada Historical Society.

A dog sled race in front of the Riverside Hotel in Reno in 1929. Brothers Dewain and Tud Kent were the mushers who drove their teams of dogs north on Virginia Street. Courtesy of Jerry Fenwick.

Snow-covered downtown Sparks, a railroad town named after Governor John Sparks, ca. 1930. A Street is in the center, with B Street on the left. When the Southern Pacific Railroad moved its enterprises to Sparks in 1902, the houses on the right were moved from Wadsworth to town. Courtesy of Jerry Fenwick.

Idlewild Park in Reno after a snowstorm in the 1930s. Courtesy of Jerry Fenwick.

A Christmas Tree Tradition Born in the Depression
Santa Distributed Nineteen Hundred Stockings

The city of Fallon, the county seat of Churchill County, located on US 50, contains a diverse mix of residents, including members of the Paiute and Shoshone tribes. Other people settled there because of the agricultural opportunities created by the Newlands Reclamation Project that began diverting Truckee River water to the area in 1906. The primary crop grown is alfalfa.

In 1944 during World War II, the federal government built an airstrip in the county and opened the Fallon Naval Air Station. Now the navy trains its pilots in air-to-ground and electronic warfare at the airfield. The navy relies on a support staff that lives year-round on the base and in the city.

The following narrative is about Fallon's first community Christmas tree arranged by a local club to offset the tragedy of the Great Depression.

After the stock market crashed in October 1929, the Alpine Lodge, No. 24, Knights of Pythias, recognized the dreadful economic situation and decided to guarantee that every child in Fallon would be remembered at Christmas. They called a meeting to discuss how best to make the holiday a merry one for the kids in town. One member described seeing a community Christmas tree in Chicago. The tree brought such lighthearted fun and joy that even the mothers and fathers danced in the streets when they noticed the dazzling tree. He believed that in the future, young and old people would remember the Knights and tell strangers how they sponsored the first community Christmas tree in Fallon.

The club petitioned the Fallon City Council for permission to erect a huge evergreen tree in the middle of downtown. The council agreed and directed the city clerk, Harrie Knobloch, to install colored lights on the tree. To further decorate the tree, the Knights solicited donations of ornaments from the town folk. The club held several dances and netted more than five hundred dollars for the holiday celebration. From the money they raised, the men spent twenty dollars for a fir tree from the Verdi area and used the rest of the money for material to make stockings and for presents to stuff in them.

On the Sunday before Christmas, the members erected a forty-foot pine tree on the back of a flatbed truck, camouflaged with evergreen branches, at the intersection of First and Maine Streets downtown. On Christmas Eve, more than an hour before the festivities started, bundled up against the frigid night air, parents and their excited children began to arrive to secure a good viewing spot. Eventually, more than three thousand people joined the merry affair.

At the stroke of 8:00 P.M., carpenter and master of ceremonies Obie Harrell raised his hands to welcome the crowd. He introduced Rev. P. Soderstrom, who invoked a blessing upon the audience and gave thanks for the occasion. Then Harrell introduced Mayor J. N. Tedford to welcome everyone. The mayor promised such events would become a permanent celebration in Fallon's future. As he wished everyone "Merry Christmas and Happy New Year," he gave the signal to flip on the colored tree lights. The lights thrilled everyone around the tree, and many exclaimed, "Ah!"

Next the crowd heard the chug, chug, chug of a truck coming down the street. Santa Claus, played by sixty-one-year-old Charles Fisher, arrived, sitting on the top of a heavily loaded gift truck. An honor guard of the lodge dressed in full regalia smartly escorted him to the tree. Other Knights cleared a path and lined the youngsters up around the tree to meet old Saint Nick.

The smiling Santa stood as he gave each child a red-mesh gift bag shaped like a Christmas stocking. The Pythian sisters sewed each of these bags and stuffed them with hard Christmas candy, candy ribbons, nuts, an apple, and an orange. Santa finally finished distributing the nineteen hundred stockings to the children about nine thirty. Because of this joyful celebration, the hard facts about the Depression were forgotten for one night. The tykes and their parents remembered that special Christmas for years and years.

As Mayor Tedford promised, erecting the Fallon community tree became a permanent holiday event in town. Today, many residents fondly recall the excitement of Santa's visit and the wondrous community trees from their childhoods. Each year they return with their children and grandchildren for the tree-lighting ceremony.

As of 2010 the city of Fallon still erects a community Christmas tree for the enjoyment of the residents and their children. Two lucky city employees from the public works department drive to a California tree farm to pick out the ideal tree and truck it to the city's corporate yard. The pine tree is stored until the city moves it downtown on the first Friday in December. When the tree is erected in December, little children and the young at heart know Santa will soon be on his way.

Santa Claus Comes to Las Vegas
Christmas in a Growing Town

The year 1930 was a pivotal time for the growth of Las Vegas as a city. The year before, in 1929, Las Vegas High School opened and the Las Vegas Review-Journal *became a daily newspaper. In 1931 the Nevada Legislature repealed its gambling ban, and the Pair-O-Dice Club opened on Highway 91—known later as the famous Las Vegas Strip.*

In the midst of these major changes, as the following story demonstrates, one tradition remained constant: Santa Claus made his annual visit to all the children of Las Vegas.

Like other boys and girls in Nevada, the Las Vegas children looked forward to meeting Santa Claus. In 1930, even though Santa's schedule was busy, he managed to spend almost a week in Las Vegas and visited at least sixteen places during that Yule season. One of these stops was at the Baptist church on the Westside, where the jolly old elf visited four days before Christmas. During that same week he visited all twelve grammar school classrooms, and one evening the parishioners of the Methodist church welcomed old Santa to their house of worship. On the afternoon of December 24, he arranged his schedule to be at the Salvation Army's colorfully adorned pine tree. There, Santa thrilled three hundred children with new toys, candy, and fruit.

On Christmas Eve, in anticipation of Santa's appearance, the Rotary Club built a platform around an evergreen tree growing downtown and strung colorful lights around the tree. Parents and children gathered at the big tree to meet Santa Claus face to face. The jolly gentleman greeted all the youngsters, many of whom were the children of the workers who had originally arrived in the city to help build the San Pedro, Los Angeles & Salt Lake Railroad. Although the rail construction was completed in 1905, a number of these families had stayed, becoming the seed population for the city. These workers were from many different backgrounds and included local Southern Paiute Indians, whites, Mexicans, and Japanese. Thus, from its very beginning, Las Vegas has had a diverse population. Almost a thousand of these tiny tots were either led by their parents or carried across the stage to meet the jolly and patient man. Santa gave each child a gift, and no matter the present, they acted as if it was of great value.

On the night of December 25, Santa returned to the same Westside Baptist church to visit the children at the Japanese services. By 1930 the local Japanese had converted from Buddhism to Christianity because their spiritual leaders rode the circuit and rarely visited Las Vegas. On Christmas Day the minister conducted the services in Japanese and English. After the services Santa distributed gifts to the eager and excited children.

On December 26 the signs of Santa's generosity were everywhere. Santa's kindness was most evident on the paved streets, as boys and girls glided down the pavement on their shiny new roller skates or raced their bicycles, shouting in delight. Some of the girls were strolling along the sidewalks, pushing their new baby-doll buggies, while hundreds of kids zipped down the streets on their recently acquired scooters. And smiling grown-ups paraded about to show off their new ties, hats, and jewelry. People frequently mentioned the delight of the Christmas season as they sauntered past one another.

Some residents saw an interesting scene in front of the *Las Vegas Review-Journal*'s office. In the Santa tradition the circulation manager gave his paperboys bags of holiday candy to relish. Occasionally, a boy lost his grip on the sack, and it fell to the sidewalk and broke. The youngster retrieved what he could, but several pieces remained on the ground.

A bearded man, dressed in tattered clothes, lingered near the group. Waiting until the youngster finished picking up most of his candy, the man dove down, grabbed two or three pieces of the leftover sweets, stuffed them in his mouth, and licked his lips as he savored them in sheer joy. Because the Salvation Army fed him, the man was not really hungry. With a sweet tooth, he could not resist the candy, even if he had to pick it up out of the sidewalk dirt.

Despite this candy-driven man's behavior, Christmas in 1930 was overall a joyful time in Las Vegas. As he would for years to come, Santa left behind many Christmas presents that the children and adults were thrilled to display on the streets of their growing town.

The Christmas Gal
Shirley Biglieri Lived for Christmas

Palisade, in northeastern Nevada about ten miles west of Carlin, was a stop on the Southern Pacific and Western Pacific railroad lines and the northern terminus for the Eureka & Palisade Railroad. In the 1920s and early 1930s, Italian immigrants Della and Serafino Biglieri and their four children, Les, Mel, Eve, and Clyde, lived in Palisade after Serafino found a job working as a fireman for the Eureka & Palisade Railroad. Later, the family moved to Reno, and when Clyde grew up, he was elected to the Reno City Council and served for two terms in the 1970s.

Clyde Biglieri's story describes his poverty-stricken childhood in Palisade and his later fantastic Christmases made possible by his wife, Shirley.

Clyde Biglieri remembers the tough times his family experienced in Palisade. When his father, Serafino, lost his position with the railroad and no other work was available in the area in the early 1930s, the poverty-stricken family lived in a two-room shack with no electricity, running water, or plumbing. Serafino sawed railroad ties and tossed them into the woodstove to heat the tiny cabin. Clyde's mother heated water on the stove in copper pots to bathe the kids a couple of times a week in the warm water.

Because his family was so destitute, Clyde remembers only one Christmas when the family celebrated the holiday. That year his mother decorated a fir tree and lit it by snapping cups on the branches and placing burning candles in them. In looking back he thought it was a miracle the house did not burn down.

In 1934 the family moved to Reno, but when their mother got sick, Clyde and his siblings were sent to live with different aunts and uncles for a while. During these years the only Christmas present he received was a new pair of maroon corduroy pants from his bachelor uncle Ernesto. After the attack at Pearl Harbor in December 1941, Serafino finally landed a permanent job as a laborer with the Reno power company. The family's financial problems eased enough that they could celebrate Christmas, and Clyde and his siblings each received a present.

Clyde's life and Christmas celebrations dramatically changed when he met Shirley Van Meter at Reno High School. They married in 1950, and he quickly learned that she lived for Christmas and all its trappings. Indeed, she was so smitten with the holiday that Clyde called Shirley his "Christmas gal." She made up for all of the missed celebrations in his childhood, creating a grand and merry Christmas every year for him and their four daughters, Sally, Carol, Maribeth, and Nancy. Celebrating Christmas was so important to Shirley that she even joined the Christmas Club at the First National Bank and saved thirty to forty dollars a month for her holiday spending spree.

Occasionally, Clyde and his family got a permit to cut down a pine tree from a forest close to Reno, but they usually bought a silver-tip evergreen at a lot in town. "Shirley could hardly wait to get home to begin decorating the tree," Clyde remembers. She favored multicolored lights and a lot of ornaments, tinsel, and garlands. On the top of the tree she placed an angel whose wings gently spread out over the tree. The outside of the house was not neglected; they decorated the yard and strung lights along the gutters.

Shirley made each daughter a two-foot-long stocking and put their names and candy canes on their socks. Shirley hung the stockings by the fireplace, and Santa filled them with little treasures. The girls still cherish these stockings as reminders of their "Christmas-happy mom."

Although Clyde and Shirley's daughters eagerly waited for Santa Claus to appear, they never caught sight of him; they just found the wonderful gifts he left them under the tree. As a little preview of what was to come on Christmas morning, each girl was allowed to open one gift of her choice on Christmas Eve.

Each child received more than twenty-five presents on the big day. Clyde watched Shirley as she spent hours carefully wrapping each gift. If the paper was not just perfect, she unwrapped and rewrapped the gift until she was satisfied that the package was flawless. Yet, Clyde chuckles, "the girls had little appreciation of her painstaking efforts, as they gleefully tore open their presents on Christmas morning."

Clyde's Christmas gal never failed to make his holidays bright, merry, and fun. She made up for all the harsh times he and his family suffered in Palisade during his childhood.

Santa Claus's Will

An Incredible Gift to Needy Children

The Nevada State Orphans' Home in Carson City opened in 1869. Its name was later changed to the Northern Nevada Children's Home, and the institution closed in 1992. The Nevada Legislature established the home to provide care and education for the state's orphans. Yet the legislature failed to arrange for the celebration of Christmas. While the home was open, many Nevadans donated their time and money to ensure that the children enjoyed special, festive holidays. No one's generosity, however, could match that of Henry Wood, who in 1931 rivaled Santa Claus in his spirit of giving. This story describes Wood's kindness to the orphans and their reactions to his incredible gift.

Henry Wood's mother died when he was quite young. A forlorn little boy, every year he wished for a Christmas tree and hoped that Santa Claus would leave him a toy. Yet when Christmas arrived, disappointment came with it, because his well-meaning father failed to understand his young son's yearnings. Growing up, Henry never received a Christmas present, and he never forgot this absence.

Wood and his father became wealthy by farming and ranching in the Mason Valley in Lyon County, Nevada. Wood was a lifelong bachelor with no children, and because of his connection to Nevada, he decided that his estate should benefit the children of the state. In 1925 when he died in California, he left his estate worth more than thirty thousand dollars in trust for the children in the Nevada State Orphans' Home. His will stipulated that the money was to purchase "useful and pleasing presents at Christmas time." Apparently, Wood had decided that the needy children of the home should not have to experience anything like the sad Christmases of his childhood and that the holiday would instead be a happy occasion. This gesture made him the all-time Santa Claus to the home for the next sixty-one years.

After his death two of Wood's nieces filed a lawsuit to contest his will and have his riches distributed to them. They claimed that the money could not be given to the orphanage because his will mentioned Christmas. The women argued that the gift was for an improper religious purpose, making it unconstitutional for the state to accept the money. Nevada attorney general Michael Diskin disagreed, maintaining that the reference to Christmas merely set a date for giving the presents and that it failed to create a religious activity. Ultimately, the court ruled in favor of distributing the estate to the Nevada State Orphans' Home.

The year 1931 marked the first Christmas after Wood's estate was settled. The weekend before, the older children of the home busily bedecked a huge donated tree in the large playroom. On Christmas Eve all ninety-five children helped to hang a bronze plaque outside the front door of the building that read:

HENRY WOOD
1853–1925
Our Kindliest Benefactor
He Bequeathed His Life's
Savings That Christmas
Time In This Home Might
Be Filled With Happiness

They also hung a life-size portrait of Wood so that future needy children of the Nevada State Orphans' Home would also know the appearance of their Christmas benefactor.

And, indeed, Wood's gift continued to provide for the home's holiday celebrations. In 1946, for instance, the Christmas fund generated $988.90 in interest. Former Ely High School teacher and superintendent Roland Van Der Smissen encouraged the forty-six children of the home that year to write a letter to Santa Claus, describing their Christmas wish. The superintendent used the interest from the fund to buy gifts for the children, spending between $8 and $12 for each child and fulfilling their written requests to Santa, when possible. He also bought good clothes that the children would not have had under the regular budget. Because the fund generated more money than he could spend that year, Van Der Smissen deposited the extra money into a bank savings account in an equal amount for each child. The accounts were added to each year and accrued interest. Thus, when a youngster left the home, he or she had a small amount of cash to begin his or her new life.

Wood's funds provided for gifts for children in the home until 1992, when it closed and other state programs took over the care of Nevada's children in need. Thanks to Wood's generosity, unlike the miserable Christmases of his childhood, the little ones living in the orphanage enjoyed a merry time at Christmas for sixty-one years after he left them his money. This thoughtful gift solidified Henry Wood in the orphans' memories and the Nevada history books as the Santa Claus of the Nevada Children's Home.

Three Days to Celebrate

Boulder City Christmas in 1931

In March 1931 the federal government authorized the Bureau of Reclamation to build a forty-nine-million-dollar dam on the Colorado River, the largest public works project ever at the time. The government awarded Six Companies, Inc., a consortium, the contract for the dam, first known as Hoover Dam, then Boulder Dam, and finally by its original name, Hoover Dam.

From 1931 to 1935, at the height of the Great Depression, five thousand people moved into Clark County seeking work on the dam, and they doubled the population of the area. These men and their families needed a place to live close by because the nearest town, Las Vegas, was thirty miles away. The Bureau of Reclamation spent more than two million dollars building a "reservation" formally named Boulder City, close to the dam.

As with all federal reservations, rules governing the residents' conduct, health, and welfare were strictly enforced. For example, alcohol consumption and gaming were prohibited within the town boundaries. Today, the city remains the only town in Nevada that has not legalized gaming. Yet Hoover Dam and Boulder City play an important role in the state's tourist economy, and Lake Mead, created by the dam, is a major recreational asset in southern Nevada. This account covers the Hoover Dam workers' first Christmas in Nevada.

Six Companies, Inc., began construction of the Hoover Dam in 1931. By the end of the year, the employees had been working in several shifts around the clock every day, with scarcely any time off. In December the company announced the twenty-eight hundred workers would be given three days off to celebrate Christmas, beginning on December 25. The workers would be paid two days before Christmas, but they must show up for work on December 24 if they wanted to keep their jobs.

In celebration of the holiday, the company erected a twenty-five-foot Christmas tree at the juncture of Nevada Boulevard and Cherry Street in Boulder City. They strung electric lights and hung traditional ornaments on the evergreen tree. Floodlight beams danced on the tree so it could be enjoyed at night.

Two nights before Christmas Santa Claus's white hair and beard fluttered in the breeze when he visited the tree to greet the nearly five hundred children living in town. The police officers routed traffic around the area, while Saint Nick distributed candy, nuts, ice cream, cake, and gifts to the thrilled youngsters.

On Christmas Day about twenty-four hundred people attended the community Christmas-dinner party in the Six Companies' mess hall. Before the meal several hundred giddy children received gifts of candy and presents arranged for by the company.

The consortium purchased an enormous amount of food for the cooks to prepare the holiday dinner. They roasted 1.5 tons of succulent turkey, cooked 250 gallons of red cranberries for cranberry sauce, dished up 30 gallons of oysters, scooped 300 gallons of ice cream, and baked 450 beautifully browned mincemeat pies. With the meal the guests drank 300 gallons of coffee and 250 gallons of fresh milk. As a special treat the diners also munched on 300 pounds of mixed candy and 500 pounds of nuts.

Thanks to their bosses, the weary workers and their families enjoyed this magnificent feast as a merry way to begin their well-deserved three-day Christmas vacation.

"Merry Christmas, Darlings!"
Old Ornaments and Glamour Girl Gifts

Gladys Rowley moved from New York to Nevada to obtain a divorce in 1936. A single mother of two sons, she wrote a column called "The Reno Revue" for the Nevada State Journal to support herself and her boys during the Depression and World War II. The following account summarizes several of her newspaper columns about her childhood Christmases in New York and her celebrations with her sons in Reno.

In 1938 Gladys Rowley decorated a Christmas tree in her Reno home with her teenage sons, Fitch "Sonny" and Richard "Dick." They trimmed their evergreen tree with ornaments she had brought from New York and stored in an old trunk in the cellar until the holidays. The ornaments brought back fond memories of her childhood Christmases. One memory was of a Christmas Eve long ago, when her parents sent her to bed early "because you must be asleep when Santa comes." Naturally wanting to please Santa, she tried to fall asleep fast. But her heart began to beat rapidly, and instead of sliding into slumber, an exciting chant danced through her head that kept her awake: "The sooner I go to sleep, and the sooner tomorrow will get here. The sooner I go to sleep, and the sooner tomorrow will get here. The sooner I go to sleep . . ." She eventually fell asleep, but later than her parents would have liked.

As Rowley's boys unpacked her cherished childhood ornaments, they scattered them all over the tables and chairs in the living room before hanging them on the tree. Mixed in with these older ornaments were a few new blue and bright-silver "Nevada things" the family had purchased after they had moved to Reno. The boys quietly hung these newer ornaments on the tree; their reserved behavior showed that they were not that interested in them. When they began to hang the older decorations, however, they started to talk in a lively way about a few of them. One of her boys said, "Oh, Mother, look! The little brass scuttle! I like this best of all. It was on my first tree. Remember?" Obviously, her sons enjoyed the family's old ornaments as much as she did.

Next, they hung the silly old horn that did not blow anymore—a treasured memento from Rowley's childhood. When it had worked, the tooting of the horn proclaimed the beginning of Christmas. During her childhood Christmases, she or her brother, Dayton, would vie for the privilege of blowing the horn to assemble all the family members for the joyous march downstairs to see the festive and fully decorated tree and the presents beneath it.

Among her favorite old ornaments was a tiny basket, filled with cotton, holding a small white lamb. As a child, Christmas after Christmas, she searched the tree for the little lamb and was delighted when she found the tiny ornament. The wonderment continued when she grew older and happily watched her boys, years later, hunting for that miniature lamb on their tree.

In Reno in 1940, on Christmas morning, Sonny and Dick awakened their mother when they flipped on the lights in her bedroom. She squinted at the lights and felt like she had just fallen asleep when she heard their excited "Merry Christmas!" and received some noisy kisses. The present she wanted most at that time was more sleep, but she struggled out of bed and managed to offer a bright "Merry Christmas, darlings!" Energized and eager, the boys could barely wait to get downstairs to the tree.

Sitting near the Christmas tree, as Rowley opened her first present, one of her sons looked up from the floor, surrounded in piles of wrapping paper and ribbons, and said, "That's to make you feel like a glamour girl." She discovered the gift was a bottle of bubble bath, and it was nestled in with other bottles of colored bath salts with a variety of garden scents. She opened the bottles for a sniff, and the delicate smells of honeysuckle, apple blossom, magnolia, clover, pine, spice, and "blue grass" mingled together like a spring bouquet that wafted throughout the house.

The boys bought their mother two other sweet-smelling presents. One was a bottle of cologne, and when she released its lovely enamel stopper, the citrus fragrance of the perfume inside overpowered all the other scents in the room, including the bottle of bubble bath. The other present was a bottle of Byzance, a fragrance of gardenia, her mother's favorite flower and perfume. The fragrance of this thoughtful gift was bittersweet, for although it awakened happy memories of her mother, it also reminded Rowley of the first Christmas without her after she had passed away. This scent was quickly overpowered, though, by the floral scents emanating from the other bottles, and Rowley and her sons joyfully reminisced about past Christmases as they admired the pine tree adorned with their favorite old ornaments.

Santa Claus and the Nativity Story
Tahoe Indian Parish's Events

One of the state's first US senators, William Stewart, introduced legislation to establish a boarding school for the children of Nevada's Native American tribes, the Washoe, Paiute, and Shoshone. The school's opening served the interests of the federal government to try to assimilate American Indians. Named after the senator, the Stewart Indian School opened in Carson City with thirty-seven students in 1890. Later, youngsters from other western tribes also studied and lived at the school until it closed in 1980. In 1917 federal appropriations led to the creation of the Reno-Sparks Indian Colony for the local Paiute and Washoe Tribes. The same funds helped to establish the Dresslerville Colony for the Washoes in Douglas County. Almost twenty years later, in 1934, Nevada tribal communities formed federally recognized governments, following passage of the Indian Reorganization Act.

The Baptist Church sent missionaries to establish the Tahoe Indian Parish, with congregations in the Reno-Sparks Indian Colony, in Dresslerville, and at the Stewart Indian School.

This narrative describes the introduction of some of the Christmas customs by missionaries to the northern Nevada tribes.

In 1940 the American Baptist Church appointed George Smart as the missionary-pastor to the Tahoe Indian Parish. After Smart and his wife, Priscilla, arrived in Carson City, they arranged for the national church to build a chapel on the Stewart Indian School campus. The single-story church with a tall steeple was constructed from colorful local fieldstones to match the school's other buildings.

The couple remained in Nevada, proselytizing and ministering to the Native Americans for fourteen years. During their tenure they and others arranged yuletide activities, including erecting and decorating a festive evergreen tree in each congregation's church. The Smarts also introduced the boys and girls to the nativity story and taught the children in each church to reenact this history. The show included a narrator reading the chronicle, with other students playing the roles of King Herod, Mary, and Joseph. The rest of the cast included youngsters appearing as the shepherds, wise men, and small angels.

In addition to the religious traditions of Christmas, the Smarts introduced the holiday's secular customs. A merry Santa Claus traveled to each church to distribute gifts to the young people. The Smarts also arranged for the White Cross Women's Organization of the National American Baptist Convention to act as Santa's helper to provide presents for the children.

Long after the Smarts left Nevada, some Native Americans in the Tahoe Indian Parish continued to follow the religious and secular Christmas traditions in their churches and homes. They anticipate the wonder of the coming of the baby Jesus and Santa Claus. They enjoy staging pageants about the nativity story, singing carols, decorating Christmas trees, and, of course, receiving presents delivered by jolly old Saint Nick.

Enchanting Pogonip
Northern Nevada's Frozen Fog

Gladys Rowley wrote a column called "The Reno Revue" for the Nevada State Journal to support herself and her children during the Great Depression and World War II.

The following story summarizes the columns in which she describes a beautiful and sparkling landscape, a white winter wonderland unique to northern Nevada.

In her December 1942 newspaper column, Gladys Rowley described the breathtaking sight that she observed from the windows of her Reno home: an early-morning fog had coated everything outdoors with a frosty whiteness. Compared to a dense blanket of white snow, this icy covering was light, airy, and delicate. She commented that the silvery frost appeared early in the morning, but after the fog rose, it left behind a

"Pogonip I" taken of the Lompa Ranch in Carson City. Courtesy of Robin Travis.

crystal-like world. When the sunlight broke through the clouds, she saw the trees, grass, and weeds completely covered with delicate spikes.

She noticed that even the nude tree branches and bushes were outlined in ice from top to bottom and thought that they looked as if they were wearing a brand-new outfit. Even the dried grasses were covered with a silvery layer of ice, like white whiskers. Rowley remarked that the frozen ice enveloped the dry tan weeds across the street from her house, changing the plants into exquisite and fragile objects. She was fascinated by the surprising winter costume that sparkled and enriched the frozen panorama outside of her house. Once the weather warmed up, like a snowman in the sun, the early-morning frost quickly melted away.

At the time Rowley did not have a unique term to describe the morning's icy covering of the outdoors. Two years later, though, in one of her December columns, she reported that she had recently learned the Shoshone and Southern Paiute tribes called this winter phenomena *pogonip*, meaning "frozen fog."

A Nevada Christmas Smell
A Pilot Asked Santa for Sagebrush

On December 9, 1941, two days after the Japanese bombed Pearl Harbor in Hawaii, Gordon Drendel from Douglas County enlisted in the air corps. A surveyor in Nevada, he served as a pilot in New Guinea in the South Pacific. This story is about his wartime Christmas wish.

Lieutenant Gordon Drendel wrote his mother, Mildred, about his unusual Christmas wish in 1943. He told her that all he wanted from Santa Claus was a small piece of sagebrush to remind him of Nevada. Of course, Mildred fulfilled his expectation, and from then on she sent him a sagebrush sprig in every letter. A pilot, he kept the sagebrush clippings in his plane, the pungent smell filling the cockpit, a silent reminder of home.

Upon hearing this story, Gladys Rowley reported Drendel's request in her column "The Reno Revue," published in the *Nevada State Journal*. Touched, Rowley also added a spray of sagebrush in the Christmas boxes she wrapped for the soldiers celebrating Christmas far from home. Rowley described the plant as the "lowly sage, sturdy to survive desert heat and cold; hardy to pack and ship for unknown days and miles." These mere bits of greenish gray jogged the memories of the young men to recall home and the past Christmases they knew and longed to celebrate once again.

Rowley believed that not many years before joining the war effort, these same men headed for the mountains to find and cut Christmas trees with their families. They likely walked by hundreds of short sagebrush plants in the Nevada deserts and foothills. With the plant growing everywhere, the fellows probably gave little thought to them because they were "just sage; common as the desert sands, unnoticed and unwanted."

She commented how time and circumstances changed the men's attitude at Christmas, when sage became a symbol of home to every Nevada boy serving on foreign soil.

Nevada's Piñon and Tumbleweed Trees
Leila Remembers the Tonopah Trees

In 1940–41 Roy Wolfe bought a store in Tonopah, located in Nye County, in west-central Nevada. He renamed the store Wolfe's Men's Shop and lived in the town with his wife, Ila, and their three young children, Jim, Leila, and Detta.

In the following story Leila Wolfe (later Fuson) recalls the usual and unusual Christmas trees of two families during her childhood in Tonopah in the 1940s and '50s.

Leila Wolfe recalls that a week before Christmas, her family drove forty to fifty miles northeast of town into the mountains near Manhattan or Belmont, where the closest pine trees to Tonopah grew. They cut a piñon pine, and her dad tossed it in the back of their pickup truck to bring back to Tonopah. When they got home, he fashioned a stand by hammering a wooden X into the base of the tree. Without water the tree would last through Christmas, dropping its needles shortly after the holiday.

The family trimmed the evergreen with bubble lights, homemade ornaments, and a lot of tinsel and placed a star or an angel on the top. Leila's grade school teacher Anne Tomany encouraged her students to make ornaments and garlands using crayons, colored construction paper, and finger paints. Many a family tree in town, including the Wolfes', was festooned with colorful ornaments crafted in school under Mrs. Tomany's supervision.

Leila's dad worked late on Christmas Eve to fill, wrap, and deliver last-minute purchases. He kept an index-card file of the preferred sizes and colors of regular customers, so when a rancher came into town to buy gifts for his family and employees, Leila's dad knew exactly how to fill the order. Leila and Detta helped out at the store and learned at an early age how to wrap presents.

Leila and her siblings were not as lucky as her dad's regular customers, though. "Jim, Detta, and I did not get a lot of gifts on Christmas morning," she explains. "Usually Detta and I received dresses our grandmother or mother made from about six chicken- and rabbit-feed sacks of printed cotton." Nevertheless, the beautiful Christmas tree in their house helped to make the holiday a joyous occasion.

Leila thought of the piñon pine as the usual Nevada Christmas tree, but a family living down the street decorated another Nevada plant for its holiday cheer—a gigantic tumbleweed. In the fall the neighboring family searched the desert for the perfect specimen. When they found it they brought their newly acquired cream-and-tan-colored bush home to display throughout Christmastime. They would stick the spiky, delicate, and fragile "tree" in a block of wood to keep it upright and trimmed it with tiny homemade ornaments and colorfully wrapped hard candy. They proudly enjoyed the tree, as if it were an evergreen.

Leila was never sure whether the family could not afford to buy a tree or the gas to drive the forty to fifty miles to the mountains where the piñon pines trees grew or simply loved the challenge of finding and decorating their unique "nevergreen" tree. Either way, it certainly made for an interesting symbol of the holidays. "The Tonopah families had three choices if they wanted a Christmas tree in the 1940s and 1950s," explains Leila. "Some bought an evergreen in town, others drove miles to cut a piñon pine, or a few searched the surrounding desert for the best tumbleweed."

Dining in the Governor's Mansion
The List Family's Christmases

Bob List served as district attorney of Carson City from 1967 to 1971, as the state's attorney general from 1971 to 1979, and as Nevada's governor from 1979 to 1983. Former first lady of Nevada Kathy (Geary) and List were married before and during the time he served in public office, and she taught in the local schools. When List was elected governor, they moved into the Governor's Mansion with their three school-age children, Suzanne, Hank, and Michelle. Since leaving the Governor's Mansion, Bob and Kathy have divorced.

This story offers a look at a few of Bob List's Christmases before and during his time in the Governor's Mansion in Carson City.

In 1951 Frank and Alice List bought a ranch in Washoe Valley, near Carson City. That year about three thousand residents lived in Carson City, the smallest state capital in the country at the time. This dusty little western town had only five paved streets: Carson, Nevada, King, Fifth (the road to the prison), and Robinson (the street to the Governor's Mansion).

That first Christmas a teenage Bob List and his younger brother Alan rode their horses through deep snow into the hills above the house to find the perfect Christmas tree. They left little sister Bonnie behind. Equipped with saws and rope, when they found a tree they liked, they cut it down and tied a rope to it and around Bob's saddle horn to drag the pine back to the family's ranch house. The boys arrived in the dark, and the next morning, in the daylight, they discovered that the tree was not as perfect as they had imagined. More than twenty feet tall, it would not fit in the house. Of course, the side on which they dragged the evergreen down the hill had broken branches and was simply a flat mess.

After that fiasco Bob's parents turned the tree-cutting trip into a grand adventure. Inviting their extended family to join them on the day after Thanksgiving, the Lists rode in jeeps and trucks into the mountains on their property to cut down a Christmas tree for each individual family. The mothers packed lunches and brought along hot chocolate to fortify the adventurers. The cut firs were taken to the barn and placed into buckets of water to keep them fresh until they were brought inside and decorated. This annual trek for special trees occurred every year until a fire in 1982 burned the mountainside, destroying most of the trees on their land.

Bob's mother then decided to create a new holiday tradition. She proposed planting new evergreen trees instead of cutting them down as a way for the family to celebrate the holidays. The family joined in the fun, and from then on they planted hundreds of trees that the Nevada Division of Forestry gave away.

Soon after the List family moved to the Carson City area, Bob's parents met Governor Charlie Russell, who was the twentieth governor of Nevada, serving in that position from 1951 to 1959. Russell, his wife, Marjorie, and their five children befriended the List family. As a result, Alice, Frank, and their children were invited to the Governor's Mansion for Christmas Day dinner in 1951.

List recalls that when he and his family arrived at the mansion, wrapping paper, toys, and gifts were still scattered on the living room floor. The families congregated in the antiquated kitchen, while Marjorie and Charlie prepared the meal. Charlie took great pride in roasting the turkey that served as the centerpiece of the dinner. Everyone pitched in to get the food onto the long rectangular table in the dining room.

In looking back, List remembers that "the dinner was a glorious event and one of the greatest thrills of my teenage years." Little did he know

May the warmth,
the happiness
and the love
of this Christmas
season be yours
throughout the
coming New Year.

To you, our friends…

Our Warmest
Holiday Greetings

Kathy, Bob,
Suzanne, Hank
and Michelle List

Governor Bob List's family Christmas card taken on the stairway in the Governor's Mansion, ca. 1979–82. *Left to right:* Suzanne, Bob, Hank, Kathy, and Michelle. *Left to right*: dogs Clark and Luke. Courtesy of the Nevada Historical Society.

that twenty-eight years later, he would be the governor sitting at the head of that table during Christmas. In fact, when he was governor List returned the favor to the Russells when he and Kathy invited Charlie, Marjorie, and their children and grandchildren to dinner one evening. The two families spent the time reminiscing about past Christmases in the mansion, including the time when the List family first visited in 1951.

After List was elected governor in November 1978, he and his family settled into the mansion days before Christmas. Governor Mike O'Callaghan and his wife, Carolyn, graciously offered to permit the List family to move into the mansion before O'Callaghan's term ended. Kathy discovered that although the house was furnished, Christmas decorations were not included and no budget existed to acquire them. She nevertheless excitedly undertook the challenge of creating a holiday atmosphere in this very large public space. Her first task was to provide the majestic and wide staircase—the first thing visitors see when they visit the mansion—with some much-needed holiday treatments. Looking for quick and inexpensive solutions, Kathy enlisted a friend who brought over rolls of red-plaid old-fashioned taffeta Christmas ribbon. The two made large bows to hang on the handrails of the staircase and added a few live green boughs to decorate the front hall and stairway. In the following years, Kathy would continue the tradition of the red bows, adding a stately and beautifully garbed evergreen tree on the stair landing, numerous poinsettias, a doll-size manger scene with clothes made by Grandma Alice List, and other decorations throughout the mansion.

The freezing weather of Carson City in December did not deter another common tradition that the Lists enjoyed while living at the mansion: groups of carolers serenading the family almost every night during the yuletide season. One Christmas the mansion coordinator told Kathy that a group of young people wanted to carol on a certain night. The coordinator suggested that Kathy invite them inside and serve them cookies and hot chocolate. She agreed but "was stunned when I opened the door. Not a child in sight, but many, many adults." After they came in, much to her relief, they seemed to enjoy the hot chocolate and cookies.

At the end of List's term, because they had leased out their personal house in Carson City, the family stayed in the mansion through Christmas to the end of December. They left behind for the new governor, Richard Bryan, and his family the Christmas decorations they had accumulated during their stay. Each Christmas the Governor's Mansion continues to be decorated by the governors and first ladies according to their tastes and budgets.

Richard Bryan's Christmas Celebrations
Unique Timing and Presents

Richard Bryan served as Nevada assemblyman from 1968 to 1972, state senator from 1972 to 1978, Nevada's attorney general from 1979 to 1983, the state's governor from 1983 to 1989, and US senator from 1989 to 2001. He grew up in Las Vegas during the 1940s and '50s. When he and his younger brother, Paul, and sister, Kathleen, were small, their mother, Lillie, was a stay-at-home mom and their father, Oscar, spent time developing a successful law practice in the state. Bryan met his future wife, Bonnie Fairchild, when they were students at the University of Nevada in Reno. They became the parents of Richard Jr., Leslie, and Blair.

The following story describes Bryan's Christmases during his early years in Las Vegas and during his time in the Governor's Mansion.

A few days before Christmas, Richard Bryan's father took him and his siblings to a tree lot in Las Vegas to shop for a Christmas tree. "The family favored a fuller, bushy tree," explains Bryan, "as opposed to a more open pine." Apparently, all members of the family agreed on this type of tree, because Bryan remembers that when they found a perfect candidate, there were no arguments.

At home the family topped the tree with an angel, and they strung the pine with candle-shaped lights with bubbling fluid in the shafts. If one bulb blew out, the entire string of lights died. After trial and error, they found the bad candle and replaced the faulty bulb to get the lights shining again. Once the lights were on the tree, the children hung brightly colored glass balls and icicles on it. For the final decoration, they set up Bryan's electric train on its tracks to circle underneath the tree.

On Christmas Eve, "We put out the stockings that our maternal grandmother, Margaret Pleasants, made out of red felt trimmed at the top in white," recalls Bryan. "She superimposed our names on the white section and adorned the bottom half of the stocking with a Christmas tree and Santa Claus." These stockings would be filled with small gifts come Christmas morning. In fact, other than on his birthday, Christmas morning was the only time of the year that Bryan received a gift. "Christmas morning was a BIG event at our house," he fondly remembers. Santa Claus left a lot of packages under the Christmas tree for Paul, Kathleen, and him.

Bryan remembers two Christmas gifts that were especially meaningful. The first was that train that the family used to finish decorating the tree. He received the toy in 1941, when the family lived in Washington, DC, while his dad attended law school there. The train became an important part of the family's Christmas celebrations from then on. The second was a bike that Santa delivered to him a few years later, after his family had

Senator Richard Bryan's family in Carson City when he was governor of Nevada (1983–88). *Left to right:* Blair, Leslie, Richard, Bonnie, and Richard Jr. Courtesy of Richard Bryan.

moved back to Las Vegas during World War II. He had asked for a two-wheeler bike. Metal was scarce, though, because the war effort had created rationing of such materials, so even though his parents visited many stores, they could not find a bike anywhere in Las Vegas. Not wanting to disappoint their son, they continued searching and eventually found the perfect bicycle the day after Christmas. This slight delay failed to diminish his joy when he received the belated present.

When Bryan was in high school, Santa left him a unique present also related to transportation. Under the Christmas tree he found a new tire for his mechanically challenged '49 Ford Coupé wrapped in a red ribbon. Decades later he still remembers the name of the tire—"Armstrong Rhino-flex."

During the time Bryan was governor, from 1983 to 1989, he and his wife, Bonnie, would host a party for the kids in the Children's Home in Carson City. The celebration was one of his favorite Christmas events as governor. Meanwhile, at the Governor's Mansion, his brother and sister and their families would sometimes join him and Bonnie for dinner and share their memories of earlier Christmases.

Today, Richard fondly remembers his childhood Christmases in Las Vegas, filled with special presents and fun family traditions. He shares those memories and the current holidays with Bonnie, their children, and their grandchildren, Connor, Jack, Ally, Grace, Emilee, and Will.

PHOTOGRAPHS

1940s – 1950s

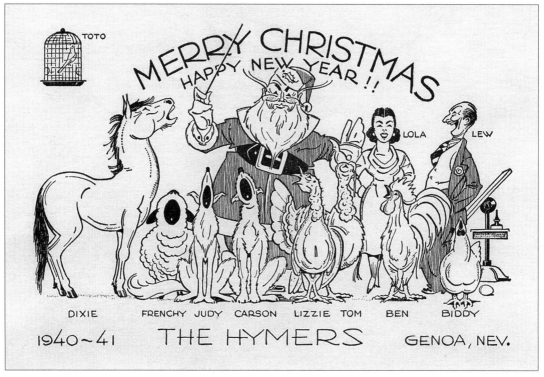

The Hymers family Christmas and New Year's card drawn in 1940–41. At the time Lola and Lew Hymers lived on a ranch in Genoa, Nevada. Lew Hymers, a well-known commercial artist and cartoonist from about 1910 to 1945, drew many pen-and-ink caricatures of prominent men (and a few women) in northern Nevada for the *Reno Evening Gazette*. Courtesy of the Nevada Historical Society.

FACING PAGE:

Top: Real estate man Joe Hall and his wife Hazel's Christmas card in 1943. The couple engaged Lew Hymers to draw several of their Christmas cards in the 1940s. This card depicts a view looking down from Geiger Grade on the road from Reno to Virginia City. Courtesy of the Nevada Historical Society.

Bottom: Holiday card from Washoe Pines in Franktown in Washoe Valley. Lew Hymers drew this card and others for businesses to be used to promote their operations. Courtesy of the Nevada Historical Society.-

The Truckee River with lighted trees on the Virginia and Sierra Street bridges, ca. 1935 to 1944. The Riverside Hotel is on the left; the Masonic Temple is on the right. The Work Projects Administration created and landscaped the island in the middle of the river. Courtesy of Neal Cobb.

The El Rancho Hotel covered in snow in 1949. The hotel, the first on the Las Vegas Strip, opened in 1941. This building burned down in 1960, and today the Hilton Vacation Club occupies part of the site. Courtesy of the Las Vegas News Bureau.

The Sky Tavern ski resort on Mount Rose, southwest of Reno, in the 1940s. The ski tow is in the center of the photograph, and the lodge is on the left in the trees. Courtesy of Jerry Fenwick.

FACING PAGE:

Top: The Sky Tavern on Mount Rose, southwest of Reno, ca. 1940 to the 1950s. Skiers wait for their turn to use the ski tow. The Mount Rose Highway was closed during the winter, and skiers glided over the road down the slope. Courtesy of Jerry Fenwick.

Bottom: The Flamingo Hotel in Las Vegas after the 1949 snowstorm. Mobster Bugsy Siegel supervised the construction of this luxury hotel on the Las Vegas Strip that opened in 1946. This structure was demolished in 1993, and the property is part of the Flamingo Las Vegas Hotel and Casino. Courtesy of the Las Vegas News Bureau.

In the Jolly
Spirit
of
CHRISTMASES
PAST
on the Comstock Lode

Lucius Beebe and Charles Cleeg's Christmas card. Beebe, an author, newspaper columnist, and railroad historian, is on the right. His partner, Cleeg, a photographer, is on the left. The men lived with their dog, T-Bone Towser, in a house on A Street in Virginia City from 1950 to 1960. Courtesy of the Nevada Historical Society.

A publicity photo in Red Rock Canyon, 1958. *Left to right:* Valda Boyne and Annette McKay, Bluebell Girls, decorating a Joshua tree. Bluebell Girls were a famous dance troupe composed of high-kicking, tall nightclub dancers who performed at the Stardust Hotel from 1958 to 1991. Courtesy of Special Collections, University Libraries, University of Nevada, Las Vegas.

A snowstorm on Fremont Street in Las Vegas in 1958. Courtesy of the Las Vegas News Bureau.

Angel Without Wings

Mother Made Christmas Magical

Las Vegas attorney Nancy Murray (later Harkess) grew up in Las Vegas in the 1940s and '50s as an only child. Although the family did not have much money, her movie-star-beautiful mother, Dorothy, always made Christmas a magical, special celebration. She worked as the Western Union night manager, the first woman in Las Vegas to hold such a position.

The following story is about how Murray's mother created merry and memorable Christmases, even when the family had financial worries.

Nancy Murray has often heard people say that they did not know they were poor when they were children. When she was growing up, she knew that her family's financial situation was precarious, but she believed that she was rich beyond measure when it came to her mother, an angel without wings. "I was a lucky child because I had the best mother on the planet," Murray fondly recalls.

During the holidays Murray's family was so poor that the only Christmas trees she had at home were the ones that her teachers gave her from their classrooms. She and her mother put up the pine tree the day after school recessed for Christmas vacation. To decorate the tree they strung cranberries and popcorn to wrap around it. After Christmas they ate the popcorn but tossed out the rotten cranberries.

Every year Murray's mother made a big deal about Christmas and would bring her daughter to visit Santa Claus at Sears. Murray treasured this special holiday ritual, in part because this Saint Nick was considered by many in town to be the premier Santa in Las Vegas. But it was more than this top-notch Las Vegas Santa that enthralled Murray as a child. Through her hazel eyes, all of Las Vegas was a magical place at Christmastime. Her mother drove them down Fremont Street to see the bright streetlights shining on the holiday decorations, accompanied by the sound of Christmas music played from loudspeakers. When they first spied the beautiful lights, they shouted, "I see Christmas lights!" They also drove by the beautiful and colorful displays in front of many of the Las Vegas Strip hotels.

On Christmas Eve Murray put out her long, skinny red stocking. Santa filled it with tiny gifts that her mother had made, plus a Baby Ruth candy bar or two. Because her mother worked on Christmas night to make extra money, Murray's family tradition did not include a special dinner menu, and she instead dined on canned Hormel tamales, a dish she still loves and fondly associates with the holiday. An especially memorable Christmas was the year that, unbeknownst to Murray, her mother stayed up into the early hours of the morning after getting home from work to crochet doll dresses. On Christmas morning Murray awoke and saw six stunning storybook dolls standing on a round mirror that looked like a skating pond. Each doll wore a different color skating dress—a breathtaking sight.

When Murray's own children, Deanna and Craig, were small, she continued her mother's tradition of looking for Christmas lights at night. She drove her children through the Las Vegas neighborhoods on Christmas Eve, each one competing to be the first to spot a holiday decoration and give a shout, "I see Christmas lights!" Today, Christmas Eve is Murray's special time when she invites her family—including four grandchildren and two great-grandchildren—to celebrate at her house. The gifts exchanged are not too important but are wonderful and thoughtfully given. "The love shared by the family on that special evening nourishes my soul," she explains. Murray makes Christmas as magical for her family as her angelic mother did for her.

A Toy Factory in Verdi

An Earthquake Destroyed Santa's Workshop

Verdi began as a crossing of the Truckee River about ten miles west of Reno. When the Central Pacific Railroad laid its tracks through Washoe County in 1868, the company established a train station at the river crossing and named it after Giuseppe Verdi, the Italian opera composer. From then until 1929, because of the area's rich lumber resources, the Verdi Planing Mill and Box Factory employed many workers at what was at that time the largest manufacturer in Washoe County. That year two fires destroyed these businesses and a section of the town. The companies never reopened, and the town never recovered. After the fires Verdi offered opportunities to those seeking a place to open a business.

This account is about the Christmas toy factory that operated in Verdi during only one Christmas, despite the best of plans.

Santa needed help assembling toys for his Christmas Eve trips to Nevada, and he found two good "elves" in Reno. Retiree Joseph Wright, searching for something to occupy his time, began building wooden toys in his backyard on South Virginia Street in Reno in the summer of 1948. In October Wright partnered with carpenter Victor McPartland to form Rex-Line Industries, a manufacturer of wooden Christmas toys.

The two men began with a few carpenters' tools, a pile of lumber, and a lot of enthusiasm. The partners chose Verdi to locate their manufacturing operations because it was close to Reno and offered an abundance of lumber and necessary materials for the production of their toys. They rented some rooms in Anna and Robert Crump's large old general store building on US 40, the main highway through town. The Crumps lived in part of the old brick building and rented a bigger section of it to Rex-Line.

The building offered ample room in case Wright and McPartland needed to expand their operations.

To assist Santa Claus in making Christmas presents, the partners manufactured and painted wooden hobby horses, hobby horse rockers, and stick horses with wooden heads. The men planned to add other toys and playthings as their business increased. By the end of November the partners employed twelve people in their workshop. Some employees planed blocks of wood into smooth toy horses, and four women chatted as they assembled and painted the finished toys.

The completed toys were trucked to stores in the Bay Area or sold to local merchants in Reno. On one of Wright's sales trips to Oakland, a wholesaler ordered 120,000 toy horses. Because the demand was so great for their toys, they could barely fill all their current orders for delivery by December 20, so the company began refusing orders by mid-November.

Foreseeing a major expansion for future sales, the businessmen hired a general sales manager, and he promptly began contacting national sales representatives, wholesalers, and distributors for a big Christmas campaign in 1949. In anticipation of the sales manager's success, the partners intended to build a larger plant adjoining their workshop and open general offices in Reno.

Mother Nature cut short the future of Santa's workshop and Rex-Line Industries, though. On the morning of December 29, 1948, a massive earthquake shook Verdi so violently that almost all the buildings in town sustained some damage, even though none of the structures was more than two stories tall. One of the outer walls of the Crumps' old general store building, already damaged in an earlier earthquake, partially crumbled, and the rest of the wall kept wiggling back and forth. Fire chief Karl Evans recommended that the Washoe County commissioners condemn the building, and they soon did.

In April Wright vowed to relocate and open a manufacturing plant in Reno, and he set up temporary offices near his house on South Virginia Street. He struck out on his own without McPartland's help. He announced plans to hire a merchandizing expert, general sales manager, engineering designer, and production manager. Wright bragged that his toy company would be the only one in the West because the only other similar toy manufacturer in the country operated in Connecticut. Despite his ambitious plans, however, and much to Santa's dismay, Wright lacked the financial wherewithal to reopen his toy factory in Reno or elsewhere in the state.

Honey Cake Holiday Houses
German Christmas Goodies and Decorations

Some Nevada families brought their Christmas customs from the "old country," including the family of retired University of Nevada, Reno, System electrical engineer Richard "Dick" Belaustegui, whose ancestors came from Germany. Belaustegui grew up in Reno during the 1940s and '50s. His dad, Bunny Belaustegui, worked for Martin Ironworks as an ironworker and helped build many of the larger buildings in the Reno area. At Christmastime his mother, Martha Lohse Belaustegui, enjoyed following his grandmother Alma's recipes from Kemnitz, Germany, where his maternal grandparents grew up.

The following story details the holiday traditions of the Belaustegui family.

Dick Belaustegui's mother got a head start on Christmas. She began baking holiday cookies, including butter cookies, almond crescents, and rum balls, in early November. She tucked away these treats to be enjoyed at Christmas, but "my sister, Joyce, and I pilfered as many as we could when we discovered where our mother had hidden the goodies," Belaustegui recalls.

In December his mother baked streuselkuchen, a German coffee cake. According to Belaustegui, in German *streusel* means "strewn about," and *kuchen* means "cake." She mixed special dough and baked it on a large sheet pan. Then she tossed a mixture of flour, sugar, and butter to create crumbles the size of tiny popcorn balls to cover the coffee cake. "Joyce and I loved to snatch the topping balls off the freshly baked cake to savor the sweet taste," he fondly remembers.

His mom also followed a family recipe and tradition to create candy houses out of honey cake. She baked a sheet cake and followed cardboard patterns to cut the cake into shapes to make walls and roofs. Belaustegui and his older sister, Joyce, helped assemble these pieces into houses by securing them together with toothpicks. The kids then covered the buildings and structures with icing made from whipped egg whites and finally stuck candy all over them.

In December Belaustegui's mom also baked dozens of loaves of "stollen"—German Christmas bread. Most of these loaves were carefully wrapped in cheesecloth, then in brightly colored paper, and packaged as gifts for friends and relatives. His mom saved some loaves that she sliced and toasted for the family to enjoy on Christmas morning.

Christmas dinner was a feast with grandparents, aunts, uncles, and cousins. Belaustegui's mom normally served a ham along with lamb and many side dishes. For dessert she served her tasty cookies, streuselkuchen, seven-layer German chocolate cake, and apple and pumpkin pies. The adults washed their dessert down with hot toddies made from rum, brown sugar, lemon, butter, and hot water, with cinnamon on top.

A week or two before Christmas, the family cut a pine tree on a ranch in Washoe Valley where his aunt Alice grew up. When they brought the tree home, Belaustegui and his mother and sister Joyce decorated it. First, they strung colored lights around its branches and hung special ornaments that had belonged to his grandmother in Germany. Next they draped chains made from colored construction paper. The finishing touches were hanging real "tinfoil" piece by piece on the green outstretched branches.

The family displayed their most cherished Christmas decoration, a charming hand-carved village made in Germany, on the mantle over the fireplace. After his mother died, the numerous pieces of the village were divided among Dick, Joyce, and their younger sister, Alma. Belaustegui and his wife, Felvia, display their pieces in their living room at Christmastime.

These days, Dick, Felvia, and their adult children and grandchildren often gather a day or so before Christmas. The German baked goodies are still part of the family's traditions. Their oldest daughter, Lauren, devotes time to producing the candy houses, and Felvia bakes about thirty-six loaves of delicious stollen as Christmas gifts. She saves some loaves to slice and toast for their Christmas breakfast—all reminders of the German customs and baked treats of Belaustegui's mom and grandmother.

Christmas at Sunny Acres
Special Treats for the Children

In 1951 the legislature officially changed the name of the Nevada Orphans' Home in Carson City to the Nevada Children's Home. The superintendent preferred a happier name and referred to the place as "Sunny Acres." By the 1950s most of the children in the home were not orphans, but were children in need of protection because of a family breakdown. From the time the home opened, many Nevadans made Christmas an amazing time for the children at the Nevada Children's Home, and these people and businesses remembered the kids every year until it closed in 1992.

The following story details how this community kindness created a special Christmas for the children in 1952.

D ays before Christmas in 1952, the ladies of the Twentieth Century Club in Reno arranged a holiday party for the children of Sunny Acres. They hired entertainers from one of the casinos to sing and play popular Christmas songs to amuse the kids. On the day of the party, each child received a brightly colored party favor filled with sweet-tasting candy that they could savor. For dessert the ladies served the kids colorful holiday cookies and yummy ice cream squares decorated with a Santa Claus imprint. Santa Claus arrived near the end of the party with presents for all, and the children squealed in excitement.

A few days later Lou and Mert Wertheimer, owners of the Riverside Hotel-Casino, threw yet another party for the children in the hotel's

Redwood Room. Special buses transported the youngsters from Sunny Acres to the Reno hotel, where they were served a sumptuous rabbit dinner and watched a clever magician performing tricks on stage. Afterward, the chorus girls assisted Santa Claus as he distributed a mammoth pile of presents to the delighted children.

On December 23, at the home, the staff closed the doors to the living room so that they could secretly decorate an enormous evergreen tree. It was so tall that it reached the ceiling. The youngsters descended the stairs on Christmas Eve, singing "Oh Come, All Ye Faithful." As they did, their eyes widened at the sight of the big and brightly festooned Christmas tree. They sat on the living room floor near it and listened as different groups of children from the home recited parts of the nativity story. One of the children then gave the annual "Henry Wood Memorial Speech," in honor of the man who, in 1925, had left his estate worth more than thirty thousand dollars in trust to the home, specifically to provide for Christmas celebrations. Afterward, the kids heard jingling bells, as Santa Claus bounded down the stairs shouting a hearty "Ho, ho, ho!" Because of the trust fund money, the merry Santa was able to give each child the present they had requested from him.

Santa Claus arrives in a National Guard jet to visit the children in the Nevada State Orphans' Home in Carson City, ca. 1980s. Courtesy of Nevada State Library and Archives.

A new elaborate decoration and gift arrived that year that would from then on appear annually in the dining room—a candy house. The house was created by Ella Lohse Wallace and donated by the Artemisia Club of Fallon. Wallace followed her German family's recipe to create a giant "cathedral house" about three feet high. She baked sheets of honey cake to use for the walls and ceiling. Once these were assembled into a house, she covered the construction with white icing and studded it with different kinds of colorful candies. She laid out a tiny walk and erected a fence out of candy, too. Inside, she installed a miniature Christmas tree.

When the youngsters awoke on Christmas morning, they dressed in their best outfits for the formal dinner provided by the Harolds Club Employees' Association that would occur later in the day. In the afternoon when they entered the dining room, the boys and girls hunted for their seats according to the place cards on the tables. Once they sat down, they watched as the employees carried in five huge turkeys to be carved. The youngsters feasted on the moist, tender birds and all the trimmings.

That year a special guest joined them for the elegant meal. Famous author and journalist Basil Woon appeared and later wrote an extensive account of the party for the *Nevada State Journal*. "Even though it was Christmas your reporter was a little dazzled by the meal, five large Fallon turkeys, and by the great heap of gay presents heaped in one corner," he wrote. "Soon, to the tune of 'Jingle Bells' sung by the children, Santa himself made an entrance." Jim Murdock played the role and made the perfect Kris Kringle, with his bushy white eyebrows, beard, and hair and twinkling eyes. Of course, Santa toted in his sack the presents purchased and wrapped by the Harolds Club employees for the hopeful children.

On the morning of New Year's Day, the kids ate chunks of Ella Wallace's Christmas house for breakfast. They then packed up the Christmas decorations of cotton snow, tiny trees, and figurines of Santa Claus and his reindeer, including Rudolph. They carried these to the attic to store in anticipation of the next year's Christmas parties, with visions of special treats and candy houses dancing through their heads.

The "Santa Spirit"

Celebrating Christmas Year-Round

Former state senator Valerie Wiener is a seventh-generation Las Vegan. In 2012 Wiener retired from the Nevada Senate after serving sixteen years, the longest-serving female legislator born in Nevada. She served longer than any other woman in both minority and majority legislative leadership positions.

Wiener's late father, Louis Wiener Jr., was a charismatic and distinguished attorney with an enormous presence both in the courtroom and in business circles. He owned numerous businesses in Clark County, such as concessions at the McCarran International Airport, restaurants, jewelry stores, and television stations. He and his partner, media mogul Jim Rogers, built a multistate television group.

Valerie Wiener's Christmas story illustrates how individuals and families combine their childhood customs and create new traditions throughout their lives.

Louis Wiener Jr. was of Russian Jewish descent. Even though he did not attend synagogue or celebrate Jewish holidays, he instilled in his daughter the values and traditions of his religious faith. Yet because he believed that the Christmas holiday had become more commercial than religious, he had no problem with his immediate family celebrating it. Thus, from an early age, Valerie Wiener learned the customs associated with this Christian holiday.

These customs were also imparted by Wiener's late mother, Tui Ava Knight Wiener. A shy and proper lady who was born halfway around the world in Australia, Wiener's mother was raised in a family of Seventh-Day Adventists, a Protestant denomination. When Wiener was a child she attended church with her mother at a Presbyterian church or with friends at several different churches. "These experiences," including decorating a

Christmas tree and receiving and giving presents, "influenced how I now celebrate Christmas," Wiener explains.

Wiener also recalls a unique ritual that she shared with her mother. After she and her brother were allowed by her parents to open one special gift on Christmas Eve, "my mom and I watched a classic Christmas holiday movie on television, just the two of us—a mother-daughter tradition honored by others in the family." On this festive night, Wiener was also allowed to stay up later than normal because "the movie usually ended after midnight and ushered in Christmas Day." More important, the mother-daughter ritual was full of love, as "we celebrated this special day's arrival with a hug, a kiss, and a smile," recalls Wiener.

Wiener remembers another instance when she stayed up late one Christmas Eve. This experience was not quite as positive, though. When she was very young, her older brother Paul decided to show her something interesting that he had already figured out: it was Mom and Dad who delivered the gifts, not Santa Claus. He forced her to stay up that particular Christmas Eve so that she could watch as their parents put the presents under the tree. She remembers that she was saddened by the revelation that there was no Santa Claus. Eventually, however, she decided that the "Santa spirit" represented the holiday, and she continues to believe in it to this very day.

Wiener currently continues this "Santa spirit" in a number of ways. In lieu of gift giving, she donates to community projects and nonprofit organizations. She then mails letters to family and friends to tell them how "their gift money" served the community. Additionally, because she travels all over the country for her work, in every city that she visits she buys a special ornament that typifies that city. These ornaments serve as a reminder of her activities during the year, and at Christmas she displays her collection in celebration of her life's journey.

Despite her brother's revelation about Santa Claus all those years ago, Wiener still makes the jolly elf a part of her life. Some time ago she began collecting figurines of him, adding a new one to her "Santa kitchen" every year. These figurines are displayed year-round, so whenever she is in the kitchen and her teal-blue eyes spy one of them, her belief in the "Santa spirit" is renewed.

Tasha's Christmases in Tonopah

Piñon Pines and Serbian Meals

In the early 1900s, many Serbians moved to Nevada because they found work in the mines in the central and eastern parts of the state. The families often brought with them from the "old country" their Eastern Orthodox religion and Christmas traditions. In the 1920s the Eastern Orthodox bishop adopted the Julian calendar, with its thirteen-day difference from the Gregorian calendar. Therefore, in the Eastern Orthodox Church, Christmas falls on January 7, not December 25.

Tasha Tomany Hall's maternal grandparents, Mike and Miruna Banovich, emigrated from Montenegro to America in 1904. By 1910 Mike had found work in west-central Nevada in the Tonopah mines. Miruna was widowed in the 1930s, leaving her to raise five children, including Tasha's mother, Anne, during tough times. Miruna briefly returned to the old country, but she decided that America offered her five children greater opportunities, so the family returned to Tonopah.

In the early 1940s Anne Banovich, a much-loved schoolteacher, married the striking black-haired, blue-eyed Don Tomany. He became a deputy sheriff in Tonopah and later the sheriff of Nye County. In due time they became the parents of Bill, Ed, and Tasha. Much to the children's delight, every year the family celebrated two Christmases, one on December 25 and again on January 7.

This story is about how Tasha experienced these two Christmases when she was a child and how she and her husband celebrate the holiday.

In the 1950s, a week or two before December 25, Anne and Don Tomany drove east with their children to the Smokey Valley in Nye County to cut down a piñon pine for their Christmas tree. When they brought it home, the family decorated the tree with strings of colorful lights and standard ornaments. The excited children thought the best part of the tree was the aroma of the piñon that filled the house.

As a child Tasha never saw Santa at her house, but according to her brother Bill, "she believed in him until she was in high school." Adding to the excitement of the season, one Christmas Eve she heard Santa's reindeers' bells ringing near the side porch. Looking back on the event, she suspects her sometimes mischievous and fun-loving father made these merry yuletide sounds.

In addition to observing the American Christmas traditions that culminate on December 25, Tasha's family celebrated the Serbian Christmas on January 7. The many Tonopah Serbians commemorated their Christmas by visiting friends and family and eating special foods. Tasha warmly remembers visiting the house of her grandmother Miruna, whom all the grandchildren called "Baba," Serbian for "grandmother."

The center of life in the small house, Baba prepared a huge Serbian Christmas dinner with a variety of foods for her family and friends. When the guests arrived, the house already smelled of the whole pig she was roasting in the oven of her wood-burning stove. The pig was the centerpiece of the Serbian Christmas dinner. The smell of simmering chicken and macaroni—a traditional Serbian holiday dish—also filled the air. All day Baba had been cooking the entrée in a delicious sauce. Meanwhile, she took time to bake bread rounds. "The best ones were smaller rounds that Baba made for the grandchildren," Tasha recalls. Along with the chicken and macaroni, the menu usually included a gelatin salad, and for dessert Baba served an apple strudel that she made by stretching out the dough. She also included a traditional Serbian pastry called "rostula," a long and flat sugary stick made with eggs, salt, flour, and a jigger of whiskey.

Baba served dinner on her big round table and several other smaller tables set up in the living and dining rooms. Tasha remembers that the special treats of bottled Coca-Cola and rostula were stored in one of the bedrooms. All of the Tomany children and Banovich cousins spent a lot of time running in and out of that room to snatch some of the goodies.

Along with the traditional Serbian foods, Baba imported other holiday customs from the old country. One of these was placing on the dinner table several short, fat white candles cradled in small glass holders. Baba lit one candle for each of the family's living male members. She would let all but one of the candles burn out on its own. The last one lit, however, she would blow out before retiring for the night. Tasha never knew why her grandmother performed this ritual.

Tasha has tried to maintain some of the old country customs that she learned from her mother and grandmother. She and her husband, Jerry, and their son, Michael, celebrate Christmas on December 25 and on January 7. They continue the Serbian Christmas tradition of inviting friends and a few local Serbs to their home for drinks and dinner of roast pork loin, "chicken and bones" (as she calls her grandmother's chicken and macaroni dish), and other Serbian side dishes. For dessert she serves apple strudel and rostula. Like her grandmother, Tasha sets small white candles in clear glass holders on the tables and lights the candles just before dinner. She always blows out the last one that remains burning.

The Christmas Flood of 1955
The Holiday Spirit Remains

Warm temperatures and a sudden rainstorm caused the Sierra Nevada snowpack to melt on December 23, 1955. The Truckee River quickly crested, overflowed its banks, and flooded downtown Reno and other areas along the river. The water peaked in the afternoon as the rain turned to snow. By midnight the water was back in the river channel. At the time the estimated damage to the city and its residents was $4 million (about $32.5 million in 2010 dollars).

This account describes how Renoites, the Red Cross, and military personnel promptly arranged for a merry Christmas for the flood victims.

Anticipating the flood, the city workers took the Christmas lights down from along the Truckee River, but left up the lights and garlands over Virginia and North Sierra Streets. They also left on the twinkling lights on the community Christmas tree in Wingfield Park. When the tree was eventually surrounded by swirling, angry water, its colored lights amazingly shone for a long time before shorting out.

Stead Air Force Base and Fallon Naval Air Station personnel and members of the Nevada National Guard and Civil Air Patrol were called in to assist with shoveling sand into bags. They then hastily stacked the bags around the buildings downtown to serve as flood barriers. The water spread for about two blocks on either side of the river, from Idlewild Park in the west to past the city limits in the east.

Four feet of water covered the airport's runways, closing the facility and stranding in town many tourists and an estimated one hundred servicemen. About two hundred people living in the Home Gardens and Airport Road areas near the airport were evacuated from their homes. School superintendent Earl Wooster arranged for the Red Cross to create shelters for the evacuees at the Central Intermediate School, north of the Truckee River, and at the B. D. Billinghurst Intermediate School, south of the river. The organization bought cots from Sears Roebuck, Shim's Army Good Store, and the Sportsman to set up in the schools' gymnasiums. Local people donated blankets for the displaced people to wrap themselves in during their stay. A Reno physician examined all the evacuees and pronounced them in "excellent" health. Fortunately, the flood caused no deaths or serious injuries.

Meanwhile, the Red Cross's canteen services fed all evacuees three meals a day. The cooks at the Swede Mathisen Commissary prepared all the meals and steadily supplied food to the homeless and the volunteer flood workers. The Red Cross, mindful of the season, even managed to serve everyone a special Christmas dinner.

The chair of the Reno chapter of the American Red Cross supervised the activities of sixteen youngsters and their families housed at Billinghurst. The kids were thankful for the food and shelter, but they expected a bleak Christmas because they believed that Santa Claus would not be able to make his normal rounds due to the flood. Helpful adults, however, made certain that the children would still find joy during the holiday.

Reno flood in December 1955. Looking north up Virginia Street, the Riverside Hotel is on the left, and the US Post Office is on the right, with the Mapes Hotel in the background. Courtesy of Jerry Fenwick.

While some volunteers decorated a Christmas tree in the school, others hastily shopped for the refugees. "Presents miraculously appeared under the tree for all," exclaimed one excited child.

In Nixon, on the Pyramid Lake Indian Reservation, the Truckee River waters stranded three hundred members of the Paiute Tribe. With the Red Cross's aid, the school staff set up a shelter in the reservation school. Stead Air Force Base and the Nevada National Guard supplied cots and six hundred blankets to the tribe. After State Route 447 reopened, food and equipment were transported to the Pyramid Lake community by tractor-trailer trucks.

As quickly as the waters rose, they receded like a wave that laps the shore and returns to the ocean. On December 24 Christmas music played from the top of the Mapes Hotel, cheering the exhausted workers as they cleaned up the murky, smelly water and its aftermath. Reno city manager

Ira Gunn begged the residents to be patient about the removal of debris and sandbags. The workers at the sewer department and the engineer's office and other public works staff had labored frantically for two days, and he wanted to give them a holiday on Christmas Day. The city workers would resume their work the day after Christmas, he reassured everyone.

Because of the volunteer efforts of the Red Cross, military personnel, and other helpful Renoites, even those who had been displaced by the waters of the 1955 flood were able to experience a joyful Christmas that year. The generosity of all these volunteers stands as a testament to the power and resilience of the Christmas spirit.

Christmas in Black Springs
Carrie Townsell's Love of the Season

Black Springs is a predominately African American community north of Reno. Before and during the 1950s, African Americans were prohibited from living in most areas in Reno and Sparks. John Sweatt saw this as a moneymaking opportunity, so he bought land and developed Black Springs to sell lots to African Americans. Initially, the community comprised small shacks and did not have running water or paved streets. Helen and Ollie Westbrook were the third African American family to move to Black Springs. Mama Helen and Big Daddy, as they were known, ultimately became the political activists who forced the city of Reno to improve the living conditions in the development.

Helen's daughter, Carrie, and her husband, Jeff Townsell, visited her mother in Black Springs in 1956. The Townsells never left. Jeff was hired by Corrao Construction as a laborer and hod carrier. He stayed with the company for thirty-four years and worked on several projects that are well known in Reno, including the Arlington Towers condominiums and the Peppermill Hotel and Resort. Carrie found work as a ward clerk for the Washoe Medical Center (currently the Renown Regional Medical Center).

In 1956 they bought the two-room shack and outhouse next door to her parents' place. Shortly thereafter, Jeff began to build a house, adding one room at a time to create what is now a spacious and comfortable home where Carrie still lives. Never regretting the move to Black Springs, she loves the quiet country with its mountain views and wide-open spaces filled with pungent-smelling gray-green sagebrush.

The following story is about how Carrie Townsell and her family and friends celebrated the holidays in Black Springs.

Carrie Townsell fell in love with Christmas when she was a little girl growing up in Tulsa, Oklahoma, in the 1930s and '40s. Townsell and her mother lived with her great-aunt Ruth Sneed, one of the first African American schoolteachers in Tulsa. Much to Townsell's delight, her great-aunt treasured the holiday and splurged on lavish decorations for her house, instilling in her niece a lifelong Christmas spirit.

Being an only child, Townsell knew that when she grew up, she would want a big family. With her husband, Jeff, she eventually fulfilled her dreams when they became the parents of six sons and one daughter. At Christmas Carrie and Jeff wanted each of their children to experience the joy of not only receiving gifts, but also giving them. They gave each youngster five dollars to spend on presents at the Mayfair Market or Woolworths on North Virginia Street in Reno. In this way, the children learned early in life the value of giving.

Carrie and Jeff also made certain that each child experienced the joy of receiving gifts on Christmas. Once the family had erected a freshly cut pine tree in a corner of their small living room about a week before Christmas, Carrie would tuck a few presents under it. On Christmas Eve the kids were allowed to open one present. When they awoke the next morning and dashed to the living room, they found a mountain of additional presents. Years later daughter Helen describes the pile under the tree as "tons" of gifts.

As a child, however, Helen was not always sure that there would be any gifts at all. She was a great believer in Santa Claus and was certain that she heard him and his reindeer outside their house on many a Christmas Eve. Yet she never saw him at their house. In fact, for a number of years

The Townsell family from Black Springs, Washoe County. *Front row, left to right:* Jeff, Carrie, and Helen. *Second row, left to right:* Jojo, Duane, and Tony. *Third row, left to right:* Maurice and Jeff Jr. *Back row:* Larry. Courtesy of Helen Townsell-Parker.

during her childhood Helen fretted about how Santa was going to get into the house because they did not have a chimney. Her mother assured her, "Don't worry—he'll make it in." And, indeed, every Christmas their living room would be full of board games and playing cards, toy guns and balls, and other fun toys. As the only daughter, Helen usually received the latest, or "hottest," doll of the season, the most memorable being a tiny Thumbelina.

Because Carrie Townsell also likes to share the yuletide season with friends and neighbors, she often invited around twenty people to dinner. On Christmas Day she and Johnnie Mae Lobster, her good friend and wife of the second fire chief in Black Springs, rolled out of bed at about five to spend the day in the kitchen cooking. The women fixed an impressive spread that included turkey, ham, and duck along with collard greens, other vegetables and salads, and a variety of desserts. About two in the afternoon, the women began to serve the meal to the smallest kids. When this first group finished eating, Carrie and Lobster cleaned up and then cooked the same dishes for the next age group. They repeated this process until everyone had eaten dinner.

Carrie first learned to adore Christmas from her great-aunt in Tulsa, and years later and thousands of miles away, she continues to share the holiday spirit with her large family and friends in Black Springs. She and Jeff delighted over the years in filling their house with noise, laughter, and the memorable smells of roasted turkey and baked cakes and pies.

Helen Townsell with her grandmother Helen Westbrook on her porch in Black Springs. Little Helen is wearing a yellow frilly bonnet and matching outfit of the kind that her grandmother loved to buy for her, ca. 1950s. Courtesy of Helen Townsell-Parker.

Nevada Christmas Cards
The Records of the Melton and Ireland Families

For many years, as part of their annual holiday traditions, friends Marilyn Melton and Jeanne Ireland each created an annual Christmas card to mail to their friends and family. Even though sending Christmas cards has become less of a custom for many people, Melton and Ireland enjoyed sending and receiving them. "I love reading the letters for the news from old friends and family and seeing their pictures," Melton explains. Both Marilyn Melton and Jeanne Ireland sent their first family Christmas cards in 1959, and each woman approached the process in similar ways. Melton continues to create and send the cards, while Ireland no longer does.

The following describes the backgrounds of these women and their traditions of an annual Christmas card.

Marilyn Royle Melton is a third-generation Nevadan. She met her future husband, Rollan Melton, at the University of Nevada in Reno. They were married in 1953 and became the parents of four children. Rollan was a longtime newspaper columnist, editor, and publisher who spent his career at the Reno newspapers.

After their third child, Kevin, was born in 1959, Melton decided that family and friends would enjoy seeing pictures of the children, especially the new baby. She designed a Christmas card that year, the first in a series of fifty-four.

Melton contacted Ken Ingram, a man her husband had worked with at the *Fallon Standard.* In his small print shop, Ingram printed that first card and several more. Melton oversaw every step in the family Christmas-card process, from designing the cover to dropping the cards in the mailbox. She made certain that the cards contained a meaningful message, were never "cute," and included a photograph of the family. The series of

The Melton family Christmas card designed by Marilyn Melton in 1987. *Left to right:* Annie, Wayne, Bonnie, Emelie, Marilyn, Rollan, Royle, Jaime, Candith, Breann, and Kevin. Courtesy of Marilyn Melton.

Christmas cards captures the history of the family over the years: where they lived and the births, weddings, and passings of family members.

Melton framed the first fifty cards, but lack of wall space ended that project. Yet she continues to design and send a new Christmas card every year. She enjoys the creative process and tries to be original every time. She looks at her fifty-four cards as one piece of art—a project that wraps her family's story into one.

Jeanne Brunetti Ireland grew up in Reno and also met her future husband, Bill Ireland, when they were students at the University of Nevada, Reno, and were married in 1952. Eventually, they became the parents of seven children. Bill Ireland was the head baseball coach at the University of Nevada in Reno, became the first football coach at the University of Nevada in Las Vegas in 1967, and later served as the UNLV athletic director and a major academic fund-raiser over the years. In 1990 the Democratic

Party nominated Jeanne for the office of lieutenant governor, but she lost the general election to Sue Wagner.

Although she no longer makes them, to create her family Christmas cards, Ireland used photographs of her children, husband, and herself. Some of the photographs were taken outdoors, and many contained a football theme or background. She composed clever sayings, poems, or

Happy Holidays . . .
. . . Y'all

THE IRELANDS

The Ireland family Christmas card taken in the desert north of Las Vegas and designed by Jeanne Ireland in 1967. *Front row, left to right:* Bill, Jeanne, Christopher, Kelly, Terrence, Kimberly, and Kerry. *Back row, left to right:* Patrick and Michael. Courtesy of Jeanne Ireland.

messages to accompany the photos. She explains that creating the cards was personally satisfying and she looked forward to the process each year. In the early years, when Jeanne and Bill lived in Reno, Harry Frost, owner of Reno Print, prepared the cards. When they moved to Las Vegas, she used a local printer there. Over the years Ireland matted some, but not all, of her Christmas cards. Yet no matter how they were prepared or who prepared them, she strove to make each card unique.

One year Melton and Ireland exhibited their cards together at a library. At the show one of the librarians commented, "Your annual Christmas cards replace the family Bible as the record of important family events." Starting in 1959 and for many years after, this role of the annual Christmas card as the family "record" was certainly true for the Ireland family. It remains so for Marilyn Melton.

Christmas Ornaments in Mina
A Prescott Family Tradition

Mineral County clerk and treasurer Cherrie Prescott George grew up in Mina in Mineral County in the 1960s and '70s. Mina, a tiny town of fewer than three hundred residents located on US 95 in the west-central part of the state, was founded as a train station for the Carson & Colorado Railroad. Mina later served as the terminus on a branch of the Southern Pacific Railroad.

Cherrie's dad, Jerry Prescott, drove a truck for Wells Cargo, hauling ore from the Basic Magnesium mine in Gabbs, northeast of town, to the railcars in Luning, another Southern Pacific Railroad station, north of Mina on US 95. Her mother, Kathlene, worked at various jobs when Cherrie and her two sisters were growing up.

This narrative is about the special Christmas tree ornaments, both purchased and made, that Cherrie and her sisters enjoyed during the holidays.

Cherrie Prescott's family commenced their Christmas festivities about a month before the holiday. Her dad would drive the family into the hills east of Mina on Thanksgiving weekend to cut down a piñon pine tree. The girls could hardly wait to get the fir tree home to decorate it. The ornaments they used were a significant part of the family's yuletide traditions, and they relished looking at and handling them.

For each girl's first Christmas and every Christmas thereafter, Cherrie's mom managed to save enough money to buy them a special ornament. These ornaments thus reminded the sisters of their mother's sacrifice and love.

Cherrie still has some of her earliest ornaments, including the one from her fifth Christmas, in 1963: a clown made in Germany of green glass balls and a rubber head. "Since he is heavy," she explains, "I hang him on one of the low, sturdier tree branches." Through the years she has had to reglue a felt button or two on him, but despite these imperfections, he remains one of her favorites.

Besides the store-bought ornaments from their mother, when the Prescott sisters were growing up, they entertained themselves on many an evening and a few cold weekends by crafting their own. They would glue lace, yarn, and glitter onto such materials as egg cartons, tin cans, and aerosol bottle lids. The girls saved these items for months to have enough materials to work with each Christmas. Cherrie recalls the fun of trying to outdo one another for the most beautiful ornament of the year. And although they may not have been as polished or as sophisticated as the store-bought ones, these ornaments were equally as special because the girls had made them.

Over the years the sisters accumulated a great number of both store-bought and handmade ornaments. Therefore, "by the time we left home to start are own families," notes Cherrie, "we each had plenty of ornaments to adorn our own trees." She and her sisters maintain this annual tradition, giving ornaments to their own children and grandchildren each year. These are primarily store-bought, however.

Although the ornaments she has given to her four sons generally evoke happy memories for Cherrie, there are several special ones that bring bittersweet emotions. After her son, Brian, died in an automobile accident in 2001, she kept his ornaments, including a few that he had made in school. "One of my favorites is the sand dollar," she explains. "Behind the actual sand dollar is typed 'Legend of the Sand Dollar,' and he made this when he was eight years old." Every year she decorates a small artificial tree with only his ornaments. "Brian's tree" reminds her of the past happy celebrations she enjoyed with him.

"I no longer create ornaments," Cherrie confesses. Still, she cannot help but look "at lids, egg cartons, and other materials as I'm tossing them out," because these items remind her of the festive holiday decorations of her youth.

Christmas Tamales
Adriana's Mexican and Nevada Holiday Traditions

Reno attorney Adriana Fralick (née Guzmán) spent her early Christmases in Ajijic, a fishing village near Guadalajara, Mexico. The village is located in the Sierra Madre range, on the north shore of Lake Chapala. Her family lived in this town of fifteen thousand people from the 1960s to 1978.

Her father, businessman Juan Marcos Guzmán, a self-taught architect, built houses and later owned a fish farm where he raised catfish and other kinds of fish. Her American mother, Julia Gail Hayes De Guzmán, owned small boutiques that catered to American and Canadian tourists.

In 1978 Julia and her children left Mexico and moved to Nevada, where she became an art teacher. Adriana grew up in Sparks and graduated from local schools, the University of Nevada, Reno, and the William S. Boyd School of Law in Las Vegas. She married her Sparks High School sweetheart, David Fralick, now a dentist. They became the parents of two children.

Adriana's story describes the Christmas customs her family followed in Mexico and how they were unable to carry on those traditions in Nevada.

In the 1970s, right before Christmas, Adriana and her siblings selected their "tree" from the mountains around Ajijic. The kids hiked through the hills above the town looking for a bare tree branch about the thickness of an adult's wrist. Once they found the right bough, they cut it down and dragged it home through the streets of town. No one in Ajijic ever cut down a whole tree; they either chopped down a large branch to decorate or adorned a living tree in their yard. "We painted our branch white, stood it up in a vase full of decorative rocks or rice, and hung tinsel and ornaments on it," remembers Adriana. "Since electricity was not dependable, we rarely strung electric lights on the branch."

Adriana and her siblings made bright pink, yellow, orange, green, and red papier-mâché ornaments or used some ornaments from their mother's boutique to decorate the tree. They also used *faroles,* paper lanterns that were special ornaments that came in various sizes in Mexico. "We either bought the *faroles* at the plaza on market day or sometimes selected them from our mother's store," explains Adriana. The kids suspended the smaller *faroles* on the Christmas tree, while they hung the larger ones throughout the house or in the courtyard. Because a large poinsettia tree grew in the Guzmáns' courtyard, they hung these lanterns on that bright-red tree.

On Christmas Eve Adriana's mother served tamales with *atole,* a warm and popular Christmas drink made with cornmeal. In Mexico the custom was to open presents on Christmas Eve, but her mother disapproved of this tradition because the kids would stay up too late playing with their new toys. Adriana's mother preferred and insisted that she and her siblings observe the American tradition instead and open their presents on Christmas morning. Either way, the children believed that many of the gifts were brought by the baby Jesus. His gifts were never wrapped and just appeared under the tree. The gifts that were covered in wrapping paper, however, they knew were from family members.

The gifts the children received included dolls for the girls and toy trucks for the boys. Every year Adriana received a new papier-mâché blue-eyed, blonde-haired doll customarily sold in Mexico. The small dolls resembled trapeze artists dressed in colorful sparkly costumes, their movable bare arms and legs attached to their bodies with heavy string. The dolls were fragile and never lasted long after the holidays.

When Julia and the children moved to Sparks in 1978, "we discovered that Christmas celebrations in Nevada were not the same as we had enjoyed in Mexico," Adriana recalls. First, they learned that Santa Claus delivered the presents, not the baby Jesus. Second, their usual traditions were difficult to continue in Nevada. *Faroles* and other Mexican Christmas ornaments were not available in Sparks, and they did not know any other Mexican families with whom to share their customs. The one tradition they could maintain was the Christmas Eve menu. Adriana and her sister, Angelina, fixed their favorite tamales for supper.

After Adriana married David, she began to celebrate Christmas following American customs, in some cases those specifically from Nevada. A decorated pine tree is central to their festivities. If they have time, Adriana and David obtain a US Forest Service permit and cut down their Christmas tree in the Plumas National Forest near Graeagle, California. They search for a bushy evergreen tree. When they find the tree they want, David wields an ax to chop down the tree, while Adriana and their children, Katie and Peter, watch him work.

Once they get the tree home, the kids trim it with decorations, according to the theme Katie has chosen for the year. In 2011 she created a Japanese origami tree with folded colorful ornaments and selected Asian-inspired little lanterns for lights. In 2012 she decided on a Mexican-themed poinsettia tree. She made red flower ornaments and a giant poinsettia for the tree topper. "The tree brought back fond memories of the living tree in my family's courtyard in Ajijic," Adriana recalls.

When Katie and Peter finish decorating the tree, Adriana adds a few last-minute touches to complete it, including hanging her small papier-mâché blue-eyed, blonde-haired doll dressed in forest green with a pinkish red poinsettia necklace, a delightful reminder of her childhood Christmases in Mexico.

Opportunity Village's Magical Forest and Santa Run
Las Vegas Events Enrich Lives

Opportunity Village, a not-for-profit organization founded in the early 1950s, is located at 6300 West Oakey Boulevard in Las Vegas. The organization's mission is to improve the lives of more than three thousand people with intellectual disabilities by providing them with vocational training, community employment, arts, and social recreation.

The following story describes two Christmas events created by Opportunity Village to benefit those with intellectual disabilities: a delightful holiday forest and the Santa Run.

Opportunity Village's development officer Linda Smith started the organization's Magical Forest in 1981. She dreamed up the idea of an enchanting display of lighted Christmas trees as a unique way to thank donors who had recently funded the construction of the organization's new campus. She borrowed a few pine trees from a nursery, carefully covered them with twinkling lights, and persuaded a few Bonanza High School students to make some colorful Christmas ornaments to hang on the trees.

One weekend that year she invited donors to the little forest. Captivated by the thicket of shimmering trees, they returned with their friends to see the display. That same weekend the neighbors spied the small wooded area bathed in a holiday glow and could not resist visiting, too. Given this attention, Smith realized that the visitors to the Magical Forest might be willing to donate to Opportunity Village. She put out a donation jar and sold homemade cookies and hot chocolate. Through these efforts she raised $3,000 that year.

From that modest first year of a few trees, the Magical Forest has expanded to a major holiday theme park. The staff and volunteers work year-round to create and build the charming event. On any given day, a hundred volunteers operate the park, creating a mystical and wondrous atmosphere for visitors.

The forest now features dozens of lighted trees sponsored by businesses and individuals, and in 2011 it included a forty-foot artificial pine bedecked with brightly colored ornaments. Once inside, guests can stroll the paths or jump on the Forest Express Train to ride around the two-acre park. On their journey they pass snow-covered houses, candy canes, lavishly decorated evergreen trees, bounding reindeer, happy snowmen, and other yuletide delights. Children can climb aboard the antique Enchanted Carousel, or they can explore the impressive Gingerbread House. And each night Santa Claus arrives so that they can tell him what they want for Christmas—a nightly appearance made possible by fifty volunteer Saint Nicks.

In 2012 more than two hundred thousand people were expected to visit the Magical Forest between Thanksgiving and New Year's Day. The ticket prices were $9 for children and $11 for adults. A major fund-raiser for Opportunity Village, the event was expected to gross about $1.5 million that year.

The organization began another successful fund-raising event in 2004 when it sponsored the first annual Las Vegas Great Santa Run. For this event, participants pay a $50 entry fee that entitles them to receive a red-and-white Santa suit. They don the suit and participate in either a five-kilometer Santa Run or a one-mile Kris Kringle Jingle Walk. Even in a city famous for its impersonators, seeing thousands of Santas running down the Las Vegas Strip creates a warm, merry holiday feeling for everyone in town.

Las Vegas and Opportunity Village are not alone in holding a Santa Run. Other cities in the world that sponsor similar events include Liverpool, England; Osaka, Japan; and Tasmania, Australia. In 2011 more than 8,000 Santas signed up for the Las Vegas event, surpassing the number running in Liverpool, the world-record holder for the most participants in its event. Being a good sport and looking for an excuse to visit, the director of Liverpool's Great Santa Run traveled to Las Vegas to congratulate the new winner for having the most people sign up for its event. In the New York–New York Hotel and Casino, he awarded Opportunity Village's Linda Smith the World Santa Challenge trophy—a silver-colored statue of Santa with a pack slung over his shoulder. Besides winning the trophy, another bonus for sponsoring the race was the $400,000 Opportunity Village raised for its programs.

In 2012, when 9,712 participants signed up to run, the Las Vegas Great Santa Run exceeded all previous records, and Las Vegas retained the title of the World's Largest Santa Run. Both this event and the Magical Forest have brought much-needed resources to Opportunity Village. A financial analysis by an independent consultant showed that the charity saves Nevada taxpayers about $2 million annually because Opportunity Village trains people to work. They have also helped to create a robust Christmas spirit throughout all of Las Vegas.

"Christmas Trees on the Mountain"
MOLLY FLAGG KNUDTSEN

Rancher Molly Flagg Knudtsen raised registered purebred Hereford cattle in Lander County. Concerned about education in rural Nevada, she campaigned for and was elected to the University of Nevada Board of Regents in 1960 and reelected in 1964, 1968, and 1974.

She wrote Under the Mountain *in 1982, and the following story is an excerpt from that book.*

It snowed the other day, a soft fall of giant flakes that fell from a windless sky upon a winter world. Along the creek the willows bowed under white cloaks of snow; the sage and rabbit brush made round white mounds, inside of which lived hidden communities of birds and mice. On the undrifted reaches of snow lay fresh tracks of the wild things that went abroad for food: rabbit trails, coyote tracks, and the sharp bounding hoof prints of deer.

I saddled my horse and rode along the foothills of the Toiyabes looking for cattle that might still be outside. Hardly realizing it, I drifted higher up the sunlit slopes of the mountains, up dry canyons until I came to the first low straggling trees. Only a little further and the pine trees were all around me. Snow was heaped upon their branches and each snowflake sparkled and reflected a thousand lights; they were more beautiful than any Christmas tree decorated by human hands.

That night before I went to bed I looked long from my window toward the mountains where the pine trees grew. The sky was lit with a glitter of stars. One star, shining with particular brilliance, seemed to hang directly over the canyon where I had been riding. I thought of the Magi with their wondrous gifts, those three kings who rode across the distant desert following the radiance of a star two thousand years ago. Perhaps the Magi passed a grove of snow-garlanded evergreens as they journeyed to find the stable where lay, on the sweet-scented hay, among the cattle and the long-eared burros, our Saviour, Jesus Christ.

"Is There a Santa Claus?"
Nevada Attorney General Brian McKay's Answer

Brian McKay served as Nevada attorney general from 1983 to 1991. Among other responsibilities, his duties included issuing opinions on Nevada law and prosecuting Open Meeting Law violations. During his tenure he issued several "official" opinions on some aspect of Christmas.
This story is about two of McKay's opinions on Santa Claus.

In 1983 the children of Nevada asked, "Is there a Santa Claus?" Nevada's attorney general, Brian McKay, cleared up any confusion by issuing an opinion during his first Christmas in office. McKay found positively that Santa Claus was real. He relied on the facts that, for years, people from around the world had reported glimpses of Saint Nick and that the post office had verified his residency at the North Pole. The preeminent fact, however, came from the children themselves. "The most persuasive proof that there is a Santa," McKay concluded, "lies in the eyes of the children of the world. The radiant glow of a child anticipating a Christmas visit by the jolly old elf speaks directly to the question at hand." McKay's ruling was a relief to the children of Nevada.

In 1986 McKay again ruled on a contentious issue involving Saint Nick when he dismissed Mr. E. Scrooge's Open Meeting Law complaint against Santa and his elves. Scrooge contended that Santa's meetings with his Elf Advisory Council to consider the toy distribution procedures for Christmas violated the Open Meeting Law by not posting notices of the council's meetings.

McKay's office investigated and found that throughout the fall of the year, Santa, acting as the chairman of the Elf Advisory Council, did indeed hold closed-door meetings with his elves. Moreover, the diminutive council members and their rotund chairman discussed their gift distribution plans to the children of Nevada without posting legal notices of these meetings, as required by law.

McKay concluded, however, that the Elf Advisory Council was a private, nonprofit organization created to advise Santa Claus on the operation of a worldwide toy distribution network and not a government agency. Therefore, Santa and the council were not subject to the state's Open Meeting Law. McKay thus dismissed the complaint. He characterized Scrooge's charges as another in a series of annual protests by a group of individuals known for their negative attitudes toward Christmas celebrations. Santa could continue to plan for Christmas as he saw fit. Once again, McKay's ruling was a relief to the children of Nevada.

No More Charlie Brown Trees
Claytee White's Perfect Christmas Tradition

Claytee White, director of the Oral History Research Center at the University of Nevada, Las Vegas, is a native of Ahoskie, a small town in northeastern North Carolina. She and her seven brothers and sisters grew up there in the 1950s and '60s. Her father, Charlie White, a sharecropper, never owned or made enough money to rent any land. Her mother, Morning Gladys White, derived her first name from her Native American ancestry.

After graduating from high school, White moved to Durham and enrolled at North Carolina Central University, one of the historically black colleges and universities. Later, she moved to Los Angeles, where she completed her bachelor's degree at California State University, Los Angeles. In 1997 she completed a master's degree in American history at the University of Nevada, Las Vegas.

Claytee's story describes her underwhelming Christmas trees when she was a child in North Carolina and the perfect Christmas trees she now enjoys in Las Vegas.

Every year at Christmastime, Claytee and her siblings could barely contain their excitement for the coming holiday. Much of this excitement centered on finding the perfect Christmas tree. "We begged and pleaded our father, Charlie, to walk into the nearby woods and cut down a beautiful Christmas tree," she remembers. When he finally caved into their pleas, though, the trees he would choose tended toward the pitiful, neither bushy nor perfect. In fact, his selections never met their expectations. To make matters worse, the family owned too few decorations to fill the huge gaps that would make the tree even a tiny bit attractive or splendid. Worse still, some years only a few presents would appear under their depressing tree. And other years there would be none at all.

On the bright side, there was always plenty of delicious food on Christmas Day. Claytee's mother splurged by roasting a chicken and baking a ham for Christmas dinner, and because she wanted each child to enjoy their favorite dessert, she baked several different cakes. These included chocolate, coconut, and caramel. She also baked different types of pie, with none surpassing her orange-colored sweet potato pie made from the homegrown sweet potatoes that were plentiful on the farm.

Nowadays, at home, White's celebration centers on her Christmas tree. "Around Thanksgiving, I put up a beautiful, bushy, and perfectly shaped, artificial tree with strings of lights and adorn it with my favorite ornaments," she explains. Although she loves the smell of a real evergreen tree, she is pleased with her artificial tree because she can "appreciate it on so many, many nights." Indeed, she continues to enjoy her magnificent Christmas tree until about Valentine's Day, when she finally takes it down. Yet during those several months while it is up, she often finds herself sitting in her darkened living room, gazing at the wonders of the colorful lights. The festive evergreen makes up for all those sad trees of her childhood that looked like the pathetic pine from the television program *A Charlie Brown Christmas*.

Winter Gardens in Las Vegas
Bellagio Las Vegas's Wonderland

Even in Nevada hotels and casinos, holiday trees spring up during December. These businesses join in the spirit of the season by decorating their facilities for the yuletide enjoyment of their guests and to attract visitors. One of the most elaborate holiday displays is at the Bellagio Las Vegas. Beginning the week after Thanksgiving and for the next month, the Bellagio converts its Conservatory and Botanical Gardens into a winter wonderland.

Throughout the year the 13,573-square-foot garden is a major attraction for the hotel. A staff of 120 expert horticulturalists change the area five times during the year, with new exhibits planned months in advance. They research various types of flowers, shrubs, and trees to determine which are best suited for a given display. They then create and assemble imaginative exhibits of buildings, bridges, ponds, and other wondrous features. Every element that accompanies the garden is also carefully chosen, from the lighting that shines on the flowers to the music that floats through the air. Of all the holiday displays, perhaps none is more popular with guests and locals alike than the Bellagio's winter gardens.

For the Christmas season of 2012, the Bellagio horticulture staff planted fifty thousand flowers of fourteen varieties to create the winter gardens. When the visitors wandered through, the first thing they likely noticed was the forty-five-foot fir tree from Shasta, California, that was covered with more than 13,500 twinkling LED lights and 2,500 red, gold, and silver holiday ornaments. Nearby, four fifteen-foot toy soldiers smartly dressed in red, white, and blue stood at attention.

As they continued their stroll, the guests passed by a gingerbread village populated by several snow-covered houses, each surrounded by white poinsettias simulating snow-covered ground. Through this wintry scene chugged two model railroad trains. Red poinsettias edged the entire display, and nearby a seven-foot brown rocking horse stood in a sea of red and white poinsettias dotted with miniature pine trees.

The horse was not the only element of fanciful fauna. Included as well were eleven cheerful black-and-white penguins. With their necks wrapped in plaid and other colorful scarves, the puckish penguins skated on an ice pond in a forest of twenty-foot snow-covered pine trees. As people walked by, some of these mechanical birds sprang to life to play ice hockey.

Next, the visitors encountered the larger-than-life polar bears. Created from thirty-five thousand white carnations, these animals also wore either red or blue scarves. Some of the bears were standing tall, but one was sprawled on his back on an iceberg in the middle of a seemingly deep-blue pond.

Bellagio Las Vegas's Conservatory and Botanical Gardens on the Las Vegas Strip decorated for the holiday. The gigantic decorated tree; stately red, white, and blue snazzy toy soldiers; huge ornaments; and silver bells suspended from the glass ceiling were a few of the spectacular decorations. Five times a year the garden is redecorated, and every seasonal garden is different from year to year. Courtesy of MGM Resorts International.

These are just some of the many delights of the Bellagio's winter gardens of 2012. Just like every holiday season, these displays were enjoyed by thousands of residents and tourists alike. This wonderful holiday exhibit is a must-see for anyone in Las Vegas at that time of the year.

Sharp Needles and Soft Lights

Ethel M Chocolates' Holiday Garden

Forrest Mars Sr., the creator of the Mars Bar and M&M candies, retired from his family's Mars Candy Company and settled in Henderson. Bored in retirement, he opened the Ethel M Chocolates factory in 1980. He named the company after his mother and used her recipes for making his premier chocolate candy. In 1993 he added a cactus garden to his operations. Located next to the chocolate factory at 2 Cactus Garden Drive, it features four acres of more than three hundred species of drought-tolerant ornamentals, cacti, and other succulents.

The following story is about how the garden is transformed into a holiday cactus garden in celebration of Christmas. A major attraction in Clark County, the holiday garden is free and open to the public nightly from mid-November to January 1.

Master gardener Steve Bowdoin plans, creates, and oversees the decorating of Ethel M's botanical cactus garden, and every year he designs a different layout for the holiday garden. Bowdoin and his staff begin testing strings of lights that will adorn the cacti and other plants in September. In October the team spends 960 hours hanging the 503,000 twinkling, colored, and clear lights (new lights are LED). At night these lights create a foggy aura over the ground and in the garden air.

Bowdoin and his crew dodge the needles as best they can while trimming the cacti, but getting stabbed by a needle is an unavoidable occurrence. With this prickly job, each of his three-man crew wears out at least two pairs of work gloves each day. In all, they use almost 175 pairs of gloves in preparing the garden. The Joshua trees' needles are particularly difficult to avoid, so the men use special hooks to string lights on these cacti.

Ethel M Chocolates' holiday garden in Henderson. The lighted reindeer are prancing in the cactus garden. Other figurines, the cacti, and trees are strung with lights. The garden is open from mid-November to January 1. Courtesy of the Las Vegas News Bureau.

The workers decorate the low plants first and work up to bedecking the tall trees. Finally, they convert the gazebo into Santa's house. To the delight of the visiting youngsters, Santa appears in the gazebo on the weekends. Parents may take photographs of their children with him for free, but upon request and for a small fee, an expert photographer is available to take a professional snapshot.

When the garden opens in November, visitors receive 3-D glasses to see certain attractions that change and move because of 3-D effects. In addition to the plants, guests roam through the garden and see holiday wreaths and lighted figurines, including reindeer, snowmen, LED-lighted penguins, and giant green, yellow, and red M&M candies. On the weekends these life-size M&Ms stroll through the garden, and many children love to run up and hug these soft, puffy characters.

While the garden is open, Ethel M sells sweet-tasting hot chocolate and bottled water to benefit the Smile Train, an international charity that provides cleft-palate surgery to those in need. Because the garden is enjoyed by thousands during the six weeks it is open, many people contribute to the charity by purchasing these goods. But like every fun holiday activity, these numerous visitors have only a brief time to enjoy the holiday garden. After January 1 Bowdoin and his crew spend about four to six weeks dismantling the lights and displays to store them for the next year.

PHOTOGRAPHS

1960s TO THE PRESENT

Governor Grant Sawyer (*left*), his wife, Bette (*right*), and their daughter, Gail, celebrating Christmas in the Governor's Mansion, ca. 1959–66. Grant Sawyer served as Elko County district attorney from 1951 to 1959 and was elected governor of Nevada, serving from 1959 to 1966. As first lady, Bette Sawyer worked to preserve the history of Nevada's first ladies. Courtesy of the Nevada Historical Society.

The Sahara Hotel and Casino on the Las Vegas Strip in 1974. The snow-covered camel figures were part of the desert theme of the property. The hotel opened in 1952 and closed in 2011. Courtesy of the Las Vegas News Bureau.

The historic Sands Hotel and Casino covered with snow in 1974. The hotel opened on the Las Vegas Strip in the 1950s and was demolished in 1996 to make way for the Venetian Las Vegas Resort-Hotel and Casino. Some of the hotel's famous owners included Howard Hughes, Kirk Kerkorian, and the current owner, Sheldon Adelson. The circular tower building depicted here opened in 1967. Courtesy of the Las Vegas News Bureau.

The Stardust Hotel and Casino was covered in snow in the 1974 storm. The casino property opened on the Las Vegas Strip in 1958 and was demolished in 2007. Courtesy of the
Las Vegas News Bureau.

Washoe County clerk Amy Harvey's Christmas card of the holiday tree in the Washoe County Courthouse, ca. 2000. The building and exquisite stained-glass dome were designed by Reno's premier architect, Frederic DeLongchamps, in 1911. Courtesy of Hartung & Dickman Studios.

Caesars Palace Las Vegas Hotel and Casino's Christmas decorations in 2005. The hotel opened on the Las Vegas Strip in 1966 and has had several owners. Courtesy of the Las Vegas News Bureau.

The Egyptian-themed Luxor Hotel Casino on the Las Vegas Strip after a snowstorm in 2008. The hotel was built by the MGM Resorts International and opened in 1993. Courtesy of the Las Vegas News Bureau.

The Venetian Las Vegas Resort Hotel-Casino's holiday tree as part of its "Winter in Venice" display in front of the hotel on the Las Vegas Strip. The hotel was built on the site of the old Sands Hotel that was demolished in 1996, and the Venetian opened in 1999. Courtesy of the Venetian Las Vegas.

University of Nevada Reno

Card depicting snow-covered Manzanita Hall, an early women's dormitory, on the University of Nevada, Reno, campus. Courtesy of the Nevada Historical Society.

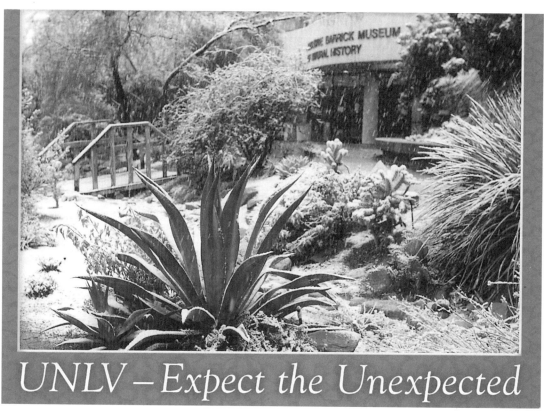

UNLV – Expect the Unexpected

University of Nevada, Las Vegas, card. The photograph shows a section of the campus with the original Marjorie Barrick Museum of Natural History in the background. The unusual snowstorm happened around 2000. Courtesy of the Nevada Historical Society.

Nevada's Willow Reindeer Herd
Children Handcraft the Animals

In 1998 "Willow Bill" Goulardt took some pieces of willow to an elementary school class in Carson City in order to help the kids create a willow sculpture. By the end of the class and after a lot of work, they had a reindeer, and the "Willow Reindeer Project" was born. Since then, schoolchildren in 180 classrooms have annually participated in creating these animals, while two hundred companies have displayed the reindeer at their businesses. Willow Bill believes this annual holiday herd of animals is one of the largest Christmas art projects in the state.

This story is about the willow reindeer herd seen at Christmastime in northern Nevada.

In September Willow Bill starts the art project with the students in certain kindergarten to sixth grade classes in Douglas, Washoe, Storey, and Carson Counties. Each teacher pays thirty dollars for classroom supplies to make the animals, and Willow Bill spends about eight hundred dollars for the lights. He buys several colored lightbulbs, but his overall theme is red, white, and blue in honor of his military family members. (His grandfather served in the Marines and his sister is in the US Navy.) He sees a similarity between the reindeer, military personnel, and individuals because, as he believes, no one is alone in the military, in life, or in a reindeer herd.

To create the three- to four-foot-high reindeer, Willow Bill and the children use Nevada coyote willows. These silver-brownish plants grow straight and slender in areas near water, and he harvests hundreds of them along the Carson River and in Washoe Valley. The Native Americans used these supple willows to weave baskets and other useful items and made various preparations from these plants to treat painful ailments, such as toothaches. Each reindeer is about five feet long and made from willows ranging in thickness from a circumference of a pinkie to a wrist. Each animal is strong enough to ride and is covered with a string of lights.

Willow Bills's curriculum includes lessons on safety, ideas of art, the use of willows in American history, the geometry of willow work, geography, and math skills. He imparts the latter while teaching the children how to measure and cut the willow pieces to make each reindeer. As he teaches and supervises the kids, the classroom fills with the whirring sound of an electric drill, the whining noise of the screw gun, and the snap of big branch loppers as the youngsters also learn how to use these tools.

Around Christmastime in Carson City, herds of reindeer "migrate" to the lawn of the Department of Tourism in the Paul Laxalt Building. Another herd forages underneath the living Christmas tree on the capitol grounds, while others graze elsewhere in town. The animals and lawns are lit at night to show off each little critter. The children who created the animals for these reindeer herds proudly see their artwork on display in town for six weeks.

Willow Bill hopes to eventually install the reindeer herds along Highway 395 for eighty-five miles, from Bordertown north of Reno to Topaz in Douglas County. In 2011 he succeeded in part of this goal, placing a sporadic parade of reindeer along fifty-five miles of the highway. With the help of the children, someday the parade will stretch as long as his imagination.

Reno's Santa Pub Crawl
Thousands Join the Fun

Reno High School graduate and San Francisco tax attorney Matthew Goedert began Reno's Santa Pub Crawl in 2001. "I was inspired after I had been working long, stressful hours at a San Francisco law firm," he explains, "and I saw two fat, jolly men walk into a local bar." When he came home to spend Christmas in Reno that year, he brought with him seven furry red Santa Claus costumes. He then convinced six of his friends to dress up as Santas a week or so before Christmas so that they could bar-hop downtown with him in a jolly group.

The following story explains the evolution of the Reno Santa Crawl.

The seven Santas, stocked with candy canes and toys, visited the downtown business area with the intent of spreading the holiday spirit. After the group of Santas gave a little boy a stuffed bear, his parents asked them to pose for a photograph under the Reno Arch. This was the beginning of an annual tradition for all those who participate in what would become the Reno Santa Crawl to gather under the arch for a picture. The seven in 2001 would eventually grow to a crowd of thousands.

The Santa Pub Crawl under the Reno Arch. Seven friends began the crawl in 2001, and now thousands join in the fun. Courtesy of Kevin Clifford.

Because they had such a merry time, the following year Goedert's six friends purchased costumes for their friends, and more than forty-five Santas participated in the 2002 Santa Pub Crawl. In 2003 even more Santas—three times the previous year's number of men and women—showed up to bar-hop. As they celebrated the evening, they shared their pub-crawl photos on Facebook, Twitter, and MySpace, including the growing ritual of gathering under the arch. These photos on social media reached an even larger number of people, many of whom decided that the crawl looked like fun and something they wanted to be part of in Reno.

The event grew exponentially, and by 2012 an estimated fourteen thousand Santas gathered under the Reno Arch for the annual photo. These Saint Nicks were joined by other holiday characters and symbols, such as elves, candy canes, Rudolphs, and people dressed in ugly Christmas sweaters. The merry crawlers purchased a $5 commemorative cup that they used to fill with their favorite holiday libations as they walked from bar to bar, occasionally singing carols as they went. In the true holiday spirit, all of the proceeds from the cup sales were donated to various northern Nevada charities, usually the local schools.

That year the bars reported the night of the crawl was the busiest of the year. The estimated financial impact on the city was $1.8 million, all thanks to the fourteen thousand Santas and their closest friends. The event shows little signs of slowing down, so in the future probably even more Santas will stroll through the streets of Reno, spreading holiday cheer and gathering under the arch for a group photo.

Elko's "Twelve Days of Christmas"
Several Weeks of Spirited Events

Elko County is located in the northeastern corner of Nevada. Its major economic activities are ranching, agriculture, tourism, and the nearby gold mines in Eureka County. According to the 2010 census, eighteen thousand people reside in the county. Its county seat, the city of Elko, is located along Interstate 80, where a number of successful casinos and retail businesses operate in the cosmopolitan town.

The following story describes a few of the special community Christmas events held in the town of Elko during the holiday season.

The first major event of the season, the Festival of Trees, is hosted by the Elko Convention and Visitors Authority. The festival's purpose is to raise money for local charities that are determined by the ECVA's board of directors. Citizens, community groups, and local businesses of Elko donate trees, wreaths, gingerbread houses, stockings, and other holiday decorations. The trees are dressed according to a particular theme established for that year. Past themes have included "Winter Wonderland" and "White Christmas"; in 2011 the festival contained more than eighty trimmed trees. The trees are then sold at a silent auction, and community members and some tourists bid on them. The success of the event is thus largely dependent on the people of Elko, and the money raised stays in the community.

The auction opens in the Elko Convention Center on the Monday after Thanksgiving with a tree-lighting ceremony. During the show the convention center is full of excited residents and tourists visiting the exhibits. Every night the trees are lit again, and the festival is opened for guests to "window-shop" or bid on the featured displays. On Wednesday night the silent auction closes, and all the trees are sold. Each tree usually fetches anywhere between forty and two thousand dollars, depending on its size and adornments. On Thursday the local firefighters arrive at the convention center to pick up the trees and deliver them to the successful bidders.

Another major holiday event in Elko is the annual Snowflake Festival. This event occurs on the second Saturday in December, when a full day of holiday activities is sponsored by the Elko Downtown Business Association, the radio station KRJC 95.3 FM, and various other local businesses. Early in the day vendors and members of nonprofit organizations set up their booths along Idaho Street (Elko's main street), between Fourth and Sixth Streets, to sell Christmas goodies. A stage for performances and entertainment is erected at Fifth and Idaho Streets, the central point of the activities. In front of the courthouse ice sculptor Danny Spangler sets up his block of ice to demonstrate his art and creates a sculpture to match that year's theme. In 2011 he carved and chipped a train to match that year's theme, the "Polar Express."

After a full day of food, music, art, and other holiday entertainments, the Snowflake Festival ends around five o'clock, and the annual Christmas Parade of Lights begins, moving briskly down Idaho Street. Warmly dressed people line the parade route, even on the most frigid of evenings, to watch the festive floats covered with enchanting lights. In past parades Santa has even made an appearance, riding atop an Elko Fire Department engine. No wonder the parade is a favorite holiday event in the city.

Then, around seven o'clock, Christmas in the Nighttime Sky begins. This is a brilliant fireworks display intended to inspire the holiday spirit. The fireworks are shot off from a small park located downtown, and they are accompanied by Christmas music simulcast from KRJC 95.3 FM. The event also helps to bring Christmas joy to less fortunate children, as spectators are asked to donate one unwrapped toy for a boy or a girl. The toys are then donated to a local charity group that wraps and delivers them to children in need throughout Elko.

In a certain sense, then, these community-wide events are Elko's "Twelve Days of Christmas." They occur weeks before the actual holiday, and their purpose is to spread the Christmas spirit throughout the town. And whether one lives in Elko or is just visiting during this time, the Festival of Trees, Snowflake Festival, Parade of Lights, and Christmas in the Nighttime Sky would turn any Scrooge into a jolly Saint Nick.

Governor Brian Sandoval's Executive Order
Message on Assisting Santa

On December 24, 2011, Nevada's governor, Brian Sandoval, issued an executive order directing the state agencies to assist Santa Claus in making his deliveries on Christmas Eve. It was titled "Executive Order No. 12" in reference to the "Twelve Days of Christmas." The following is his executive order.

Executive Order No. 12:
Providing a State Plan for the Visit of Saint Nicholas

WHEREAS, children throughout the Silver State are anxiously awaiting the annual visit of Saint Nicholas, also known as Kris Kringle, also known as Santa Claus, also known as a Right Jolly Old Elf; and

WHEREAS, the stockings are hung by the chimney with care and it is therefore in the interest of Nevada's children, as well as their parents and guardians, that the State of Nevada ensure an orderly and efficient means of carrying out the annual delivery of toys, candy, and other gifts; and

WHEREAS, numerous state agencies, programs, and services may rightfully play a role in guaranteeing that the prancing and pawing of each little hoof shall proceed as generations of children have believed it should; and

WHEREAS, Article 5, Section 1 of the Nevada Constitution provides that, "The Supreme Power of this State shall be vested in a Chief Magistrate who shall be Governor of the State of Nevada"; and

BESIDES, it's almost the night before Christmas.

NOW, THEREFORE, by the authority vested in me as Governor by the Constitution and laws of the State of Nevada, I hereby instruct the members of my Cabinet as follows:

Christmas card of the Governor's Mansion in Carson City. Courtesy of the Nevada Historical Society.

The Nevada National Guard shall clear the airspace over Nevada for the safe passage of one (1) miniature sleigh and eight (8) tiny reindeer, driven by one (1) driver so lively and quick.

The Office of Veterans Services shall arrange benefits as appropriate and provide an Honor Guard befitting the stature of a visiting dignitary the caliber of Saint Nicholas, the patron saint of sailors.

The Departments of Agriculture and Wildlife shall ensure no creatures are stirring on the night before Christmas, not even a mouse; and these Departments shall further ensure the safe passage of reindeer not indigenous to this state, even if said reindeer are unvaccinated and bear no brand, tag, or other identifying mark.

The Department of Public Safety shall ensure safe passage into homes as appropriate for a plump figure dressed all in fur, from his head to his foot; and in the event of any mishap, the Department of Corrections may not detain this particular elf from his work; further, no warning shall be issued to the driver of said sleigh should he be observed talking on a hand-held cellular device or sending text message to his workshop; similarly no citation shall be issued if the driver in question fails to wear his seat belt as required by state law.

The Departments of Business and Industry, Motor Vehicle, Taxation, and Transportation shall not hinder or otherwise impair the passage of this important vehicle, or its contents, due to any failure to procure a proper license, permit, or other charter.

The Department of Education and the Nevada System of Higher Education shall encourage learners of all ages to enjoy visions of sugar plums and other kind thoughts at this time of year. In addition, the Department of Employment, Training and Rehabilitation shall provide workforce training to seasonally-employed elves.

The Nevada Office of Energy is charged (pardon the pun) with providing adequate and energy-efficient lighting for safe house-top landings in the event of inclement weather.

The Department of Conservation and Natural Resources shall provide a sufficient supply of coal, just in case.

The Department of Health and Human Services shall see to the continued good health and welfare of Saint Nicholas during his visit, despite what surely must be a propensity for heart disease.

The Governor's Office of Economic Development and Department of Tourism and Cultural Affairs, together with the Native American Tribes, will make the delegation from the North Pole welcome in our state, conferring appropriate gifts, to include cookies and milk, and providing other abatements properly related thereto.

The Department of Administration shall make such appropriations of good will and good cheer as are necessary for the Cabinet to carry out this order, and shall ensure the facilities, personnel, and information technology of this State are ready to ensure that Saint Nicholas soon shall be here.

BE IT FURTHER ORDERED, Merry Christmas to all, and to all a good night.

IN WITNESS WHEREOF, I have hereunto set my hand and caused the Great Seal of the State of Nevada to be affixed at the State Capitol in Carson City, the day before the night before Christmas, in the year two thousand eleven.

Signed by Brian Sandoval
Governor of the State of Nevada
By the Governor

Signed by Rudolph Rednose
Secretary of Sleighs

A Few Additional Nevada Holiday Events

- Christmas on the Comstock in Virginia City

- Sparks hometown Christmas parade and parades in North Las Vegas and Shopper's Square in Reno

- Henderson's Winterfest at the Henderson Events Plaza, including a program and parade

- Lake's Festival of Lights (boat parade) at Lake East and Lake Sahara Drives in Las Vegas

- Night of Lights at St. Jude's Ranch for Children, Boulder City

- Pahrump community tree-lighting ceremony

- Polar Express Train rides on the Northern Nevada Railway in Ely

- Reno Elks' Uncle Dan's Dinner

- Santa Train at the Nevada State Railroad Museum in Carson City

- The Venetian and Palazzo's "Winter in Venice," with forty-nine days of skating on the "ice" rink

- The Cosmopolitan of Las Vegas's Boulevard Pool converted to an ice rink surrounded by fire pits, picnic tables, and Adirondack chairs

- Las Vegas Motor Speedway's Glittering Lights

Index

Page numbers in *italics* refer to illustrations.

Adams, Brewster, 17–18, 20
Adelson, Sheldon, *155*
African American community, 129–30, *131, 132*
Anker (Bendure), Phyllis, 65–67
Austin, 16

Bailey, Abel, 40–43
Battle Mountain, 21
Beebe, Lucius, *110*
Belaustegui, Dick, 117–19
Bellagio Las Vegas, 147–48, *149*
Bendure, Phyllis (née Anker), 65–67
Biglieri, Clyde and Shirley, 81–83
Black Springs, 129–30, *131, 132*
Boulder City, 86–87, 173
Boulder Dam (Hoover Dam), 86
Bowdoin, Steve, 150, 153
Brown, Arthur, 40–43
Brown, Mrs. Hugh (Marjorie), 26–27
Browne, Charles Farrar (Artemus Ward), 14–16
Bryan, Richard, 48, 99–100, *101,* 102
Bureau of Reclamation, 86
Butler, Jim, 25
Byrne, Father, 44–46

Carlin, 21
Carson City, 38, 46–48, *49,* 50, *56,* 63, 65, 67–70, 83–85, *92,* 96–102, 119, *120,* 121, *154,* 163–64, 169, *170,* 171–72
Christmas cards, 49, *104, 105,* 133, *134, 135,* 136, *157, 161, 170*
Christmas in the Night Time Sky, 168
churches: Baptist, 17, 80, 90–91; Catholic, 13, 43–44, *45,* 46, 61; Congregational, 24–25, 44–46; Eastern Orthodox, 124; Episcopal, 13, 24, 61; Methodist, 23–24, 66, 79; Methodist Episcopal, 13; Presbyterian, 13, 61, *62,* 122; Seventh-Day Adventist, 122; Tahoe Indian Parish, 90–91
Churchill County, 77–79
Clark, William, 37
Clark County, 37–39, 79–81, 86–87, 122–23, 141–43, 146–47, 150, *151,* 152, 162
Cleeg, Charles, *110*
Clemens, Samuel (Mark Twain), 14–16
Cooper, Josephine, 53–54

Davis, Sam, 4
Dayton, 54–55
Diskin, Michael, 84
Douglas County, 90, 93, 163–64
Drendel, Gordon, 93–94
Dresslerville, 90

earthquake, 116

Elko Convention and Visitors Authority, 167
Elko County, 53–54, *154,* 167–68
Elks, 39, 42, 46, 173
Ely, 40–43, 57, 85, 173
Ethel M Chocolates, 150, *151,* 152
Esmeralda County, 28, 50–52
Eureka County, *36,* 60–65, 167

Fallon, 77–79, 121
Fallon Naval Air Station, 77, 127
Ferris, George Washington Gale, Sr., 46–47, 50
Festival of Trees, 167–68
flood, 126–27, *128,* 129
Fralick, Adriana (née Guzmán), 138–40
Fraternal Order of Eagles, 37–38, 46
Fuetsch, Alice (née Harrington), 28
Fuson, Leila (née Wolfe), 94–96

Gabbs, 136
George, Cherrie (née Prescott), 136–38
Goedert, Matthew, 164, *165,* 166
Golconda, 21–22
Goldfield, 50–52, *74*
Gold Hill, 13, *30*
Goulardt, "Willow Bill," 163–64
governors: Richard Bryan, 48–49, 99–100, *101,* 102; Richard Kirman, 47; Bob List, 96–97,

98, 99; Bob Miller, 50; Mike O'Callaghan, 48, 98; Charlie Russell, 55, *56,* 97–98; Brian Sandoval, 169–72; Grant Sawyer, *154;* John Sparks, *31,* 43, *76*
Grace, Bishop Thomas, 43–44, 46
Great Depression, 77–79, 86, 88, 91
Guild, Clark, 55, 57
Guzmán (Fralick), Adriana, 138–40

Hall, Tasha (née Tomany), 124–26
Harkess, Nancy (née Murray), 113–14
Harolds Club, 121
Harrington (Fuetsch), Alice, 28
Henderson, 150, *151,* 152, 173
Hilts, Ruth, *30*
Hoover Dam, 86
hotels: Bellagio Las Vegas, 147–48, *149;* Caesars Palace Las Vegas Hotel and Casino, *158;* Cosmopolitan, 173; El Rancho Hotel, *107;* Flamingo Hotel and Casino, *109;* Goldfield Hotel, *74;* Gold Hill Hotel, *30;* Hilton Vacation Club, *107;* Hotel Golden, 31; Hotel Las Vegas, 37; International Hotel, 12, *15,* 16; Luxor Hotel Casino, *159;* Mapes Hotel and Casino, *128;* Riverside Hotel and Casino, *75, 106,* 119–20, *128;* Sahara Hotel and Casino, *155;* Sands Hotel and Casino, *155, 160;* Stardust Hotel and Casino, *111, 156;* Venetian Las Vegas Resort-Hotel-Casino, *155, 160,* 173
Hughes, Howard, *155*
Humboldt County, 20–23, 63
Hymers, Lew, *104, 105*

Ireland, Bill and Jeanne, 133–36

Jacobsen, Harold, 63–65

Jarbidge, 53–54

Kerkorian, Kirk, *155*
Kirman, Richard, 47
Knights of Pythias, 77–78
Knudtsen, Molly, 143–44

Lander County, 143–44
Las Vegas, 37, *38,* 39, 79–81, 86, 99–102, *108, 112,* 113–14, 122–23, 135–36, 141–43, 146–49, *155, 156, 158, 159, 162,* 173
Las Vegas Great Santa Run, 141–43
Las Vegas Motor Speedway, 173
Las Vegas Strip, 79, *107,* 114, *149, 155, 156, 158, 159, 160*
Laxalt, Paul, 67
Laxalt, Robert, 67–70
Leisure Hour Club, 47, 50
List, Bob and Kathy, 96–97, *98,* 99
Lovelock, 65–67
Lyon County, 54–57, 65, *72, 73,* 84

Magical Forest, 141–43
Manogue, Bishop Patrick, 13
Mars, Forrest, Sr., 150
Marsh, Billy, 50
McDonald, Fred, 40–43
McKay, Brian, 144–45
McPartland, Victor, 115–16
Means, C. L., 44–46
Melton, Rollan and Marilyn, 133–36
Mighels, Henry and Nellie, 4
Miller, Bob, 50
Mina, 136–38
Mineral County, 136–38
mines: Basic Magnesium, Inc., 136; Giroux Consolidated Copper Mines Company, 40–43; Pittsburgh Silver Peak Gold Mining Company, 28
Murray (Harkess), Nancy, 113–14

Native American tribes, 163;

Paiute, 77, 80, 90, 93, 128; Shoshone, 77, 90; Washoe, 90
Nevada National Guard, *120,* 127–28
Nevada State Orphans' Home, 83–85, 102, 119–21
Nevada Territory, 11–14
Newlands Reclamation Project, 77
newspapers: *Carson City Daily Appeal,* 48; *Ely Weekly Mining Expositor,* 42; *Eureka Sentinel,* 62; *Fallon Standard,* 133; *Las Vegas Review Journal,* 79–80; *Nevada Appeal,* 4; *Nevada State Journal,* 87, 91, 121; *Reno Evening Gazette,* 104; *Territorial Enterprise,* 16; *Virginia City Chronicle,* 4; *Virginia Evening Bulletin,* 11
Nixon, 128
Norcross, Frank, 19
Nye County, 25–27, *31, 32,* 94–96, 124–26

O'Callaghan, Mike, *26,* 48, 98
Olds, Sheldon, 57–60
Opportunity Village, 141–43

Pahrump, 173
Palisade, 81–83
Parade of Lights, 168
Pershing County, 65–67
Pioche, 4
pogonip, 91, *92,* 93
Prescott (George), Cherrie, 136–38
Pyramid Lake Indian Reservation, 128

railroads: Carson & Colorado Railroad, 136; Central Pacific Railroad, 20, 23, 65, 115; Eureka & Palisade Railroad, 81–82; Nevada Copper Belt Railroad, 73; Northern Nevada Railway, 173; San Pedro, Los Angeles &

Salt Lake Railroad, 37; Southern Pacific Railroad, 76, 81, 136; Tonopah & Goldfield Railroad, 50, 52; Virginia & Truckee Railroad, 47–48; Western Pacific Railroad, 81
Red Cross, 126–29
Reno, 16–17, *18*, 19–20, 23–25, *31, 35*, 43–46, *75, 76*, 81–83, 87–89, *104*, *108*, 115–17, 119–20, 126–27, *128*, 129, 135, *161*, 164, *165*, 166, 173
Reno-Sparks Indian Colony, 90
Riverside Hotel and Casino, *75*, *106*, 119–20, *128*
Roberts, Edwin, 19
Rogers, Jim, 122
Rotary Club, 80
Rowley, Gladys, 87–89, 91–94
Russell, Charlie and Marjorie, 55, *56*, 97–98

Salvation Army, 79
Sandoval, Brian, 169, *170*, 171–72
Santa Pub Crawl, 164–66
Sawyer, Grant, *154*
Serbians, 124–26
Silver Peak, 28
Six Companies, Inc., 86–87
Smart, George and Priscilla, 90–91
Smith, Linda, 141
Snowflake Festival, 168
Sparks, *76*, 129, 138, 140, 173
Sparks, John, *31*, 43, *76*
St. Thomas Aquinas Church, 43–44, *45*, 46
Stead Air Force Base, 127–28

Stewart, William, 90
Stewart Indian School, 90–91
Stimler, Harry, 50
Storey County, 4, 11–16, *30*, 163
Stovall, Wanda, 50–52
Sunderland, Miss, 44–45
Sunny Acres (Nevada State Orphans' Home), 83–85, 102, 119–21
Swallow, Richard and Matilda, 57–59

Tahoe Indian Parish, 90–91
Tedford, J. N., 78
Thompson, Jacquelyn, 52
Tomany, Anne, 95, 124
Tomany (Hall), Tasha, 124–26
Tonopah, 25, *26*, 27, *33, 34*, 94–96, 124–26
Townsell, Helen, 130, *131, 132*
Townsell, Jeff and Carrie, 129–30, *131*, 132
Travis, Robin, *92*
Truckee River, 16, 19, *35, 45, 106*, 115, 126–29
Tubman, Father Thomas, 43–44, 46
Twain, Mark (Samuel Clemens), 14, 16
Twentieth Century Club, 119

Unionville, 20–23
University of Nevada, Las Vegas, 135, 146, *162*
University of Nevada, Reno, 44, 100, 117, 133, 135, 138, *161*

US senators: Richard Bryan, 48–48, 99–100, *101*, 102; William Clark, 37; Paul Laxalt, 67; William Stewart, 90

Van Der Smissen, Roland, 85
Verdi, 17, 115–17
Virginia City, 11–16, *104, 110*, 173

Wallace, Ella Lohse, 121
Ward, Artemus (Charles Farrar Browne), 14–16
wars: Civil War, 12, 20; World War I, 17–18, 39; World War II, 77, 82, 88, 91, 93–94, 101
Washoe County, 18–19, 24, 115–19, *157, 161*, 163–66
Wertheimer, Lou and Mert, 119–20
Westbrook, Ollie and Helen, 129, *132*
Whitaker, Bishop Ozi, 13
White, Claytee, 146–47
White Pine County, 40–43, 57–60
Wiener, Valerie, 122–23
"Willow Bill" (Goulardt), 163–64
Winnemucca, 20–22
Winnemucca, Chief, 20
Wolfe (Fuson), Leila, 94–96
Wood, Henry, 84–85, 120
Wooster, Earl, 127
Wright, Joseph, 115–17

Yerington, 54–57
Yule Missa, 64–65